PYTHON FOR BEGINNERS

THE ULTIMATE GUIDE TO LEARN PYTHON, THE SECRETS OF MACHINE LANGUAGE LEARNING, DATA SCIENCE ANALYSIS AND DATA ANALYTICS, CODING LANGUAGE FOR BEGINNERS.

licensed professional before attempting any techniques outlined in this book.

By reading this document, the reader agrees that under no circumstances is the author responsible for any losses, direct or indirect, which are incurred as a result of the use of information contained within this document, including, but not limited to, errors, omissions, or inaccuracies.

Introduction

Python - a language named after Monty Python. A programming language that has taken the world by storm. The applications we have seen so far, the examples we have discovered, and the future prospects of the language, when combined, point out one thing for sure. If you are a programmer, Python is your ticket to the future.

When learning a new language, there will always be challenges. There will be times where you might even be frustrated and call it a day. The thing to remember here is this: many others have gone through this road just like you. Some have gone on to become successful while others have remained within the shadow of someone else. It is up to you to grab the opportunity and become a programmer that is unique and different, and learning Python is just a part of the journey. Through Python, you will be able to do so much more than just design 2D snake games.

Python has paved the way for many success stories and has certainly become the most popular language. Now you know why! It is time for you to add Python to your resume and deliver results in the most effective and efficient manner possible. Good luck and have a great programming journey ahead!

Before we look into Python, let's talk about the alternatives we can use for programming.

The C Family

UNIX is arguably the first operating system that was widely used across different computer systems. AT&T Bell Laboratories developed the operating system for minicomputers in the late 1960s based upon a language that we now call the C language. AT&T forced companies using Bell systems to use UNIX which meant UNIX was ported to various different computer systems along with the C language. Because the C language became so common, many languages that were developed later provided a similar coding environment to make it easier for C language programmers to use them.

The list of C-family programming languages is a long one, but some became more famous than others. C,

C++ and C# are the three most popular, closely followed by Objective C.

Advantages

• As of October 2019, C is the most widely used language family after Java and Python. Embedded systems and operating systems still depend heavily on C language

• Every programmer should learn at least one of the C, C++ or C# languages to understand what happens in the background during program execution

Disadvantages

• It is difficult to learn as it forces programmer to focus on things that modern programming languages take care of automatically

• The syntax, although it inspired a lot of other languages, is very ugly.

• A lot of extraneous lines of codes are required to even perform the most basic tasks.

Java Platform

Thanks to the millions of web applications developed using the language, Java is possibly the most widely used programming language in the world. Released as a core component of the Java platform in 1995 by Sun Microsystems, it enabled applications built using Java to run on any computer system that has Java Virtual Machine (JVM). Although it has a syntax similar to C and C++ languages, it doesn't demand low-level considerations from the programmers. Oracle has acquired Sun Microsystems and now manages Java platform.

For years, Microsoft's C# and Sun's Java remained in a cold war, each trying to outdo the other programming language. Both languages were heavily criticized for adding new features just to win a competition instead of following a standard direction. It was not until 2004 that both languages took to separate ways and developed into the unique languages as we know them today.

Even then, Java remains the top programming language in the world and Java platform runs on almost every laptop, game console, data center, and even supercomputers.

Advantages

• Java frees the programmer from computer dependencies and offers a vast degree of freedom

• Java is compatible with almost all computer systems. It means almost every program created using Java language will run on all those systems without any issues.

Disadvantages

• There have been serious security issues with Java over the years. Severe security vulnerabilities were found in the last Java version and Oracle advised every Java user to update to the latest version.

• Java programs are known to be slower than the competition even though there have been huge performance improvements in recent versions.

• For a long time Java remained a proprietary platform. Even after Sun previously declared it open-source, a long copyright battle ensued between Oracle and Google over the use of Java in Google's Android.

Python is Different

We have briefly discussed the best options we have if we don't want to use Python. They are great options but before you jump ship, let me tell you why I chose Python over others.

● Python is one of the easiest high-level programming languages to learn. It means the time it takes from setup to coding programs is very short.

● Code written in Python is easier to understand. It enables programmers to consult codes written by other programmers to adapt for their project.

● Python is an interpreter language. Code is executed one line at a time which makes debugging easier for beginners.

● Python code can run on any computer no matter if it's Windows, Linux, UNIS, or a macOS based system.

● Python has a vast standard library that provides methods for unique project requirements.

- Python supports various coding paradigms including Object Oriented Programming (OOP) and functional programming.

- Python programming language is free and open source. This has helped create an active programmer community and detailed tutorials are available for free on the Internet.

- The open source nature of the language has also enabled many programmers to extend Python capabilities by writing special libraries. These libraries are available on the Internet free of charge for everyone's use.

- It's very easy to create Graphical User Interface (GUI) through Python.

- One of the biggest advantages of Python is its ability to integrate with different programming languages. You can import a specific library and start coding in a completely different language and Python will understand the codes. Python supports extended integration with C++ and Java. Not only that, Python code can be placed inside a code written with another programming language.

These are the general advantages of Python over other programming languages. Depending upon your project, Python might be able to provide even more benefits. We are going to see how Python makes data analysis easy.

Advantages of Using Python in Data Analysis

Strong with Strings

Python has a special place for strings. There are multiple string related operations supported by Python. These operations are a big help in data analysis stages of parsing and processing if you are dealing with string data.

Dedicated Libraries

There are dedicated libraries in Python that help make data analysis projects easier to handle. The libraries are regularly updated which means they are compatible with the latest analysis algorithms.

Some of the popular data analysis libraries available on Python are:

1. NumPy: Collection of mathematical functions for fast calculations

2. SciPy: Offers advanced scientific tools

3. Pandas: Offers robust handling of mathematical components using data structures

4. Matplotlib: Offers data visualization methods including line plots, bar charts, and scatter plots.

Highly Scalable

Python is very efficient in handling large and complex datasets. This quality has made this programming language invaluable to companies like YouTube, Facebook, and Amazon that deal with huge data on a consistent basis.

Fast Deployment

With a simple coding syntax and straightforward development process, it's definitely faster to create and deploy applications using Python as compared to other languages.

If you look at the larger picture, Python provides the easiest yet most robust coding environment. It's faster to learn and deploy applications. It integrates well with other programming languages and technologies. There are tons of free tutorials and documentations available online for help if you are not able to resolve an issue.

All of the above qualities make Python the best package when it comes to programming languages. Yes, you might find that another programming language suits your needs better for a specific application, for example, for web applications JavaScript is more popular, and for database, SQL is used more. But, as a whole, Python offers you everything you need for 90% of the programming tasks.

Knowing all this, do you still think I made a mistake sticking with Python? Personally, I think it was a great decision. I told my friend all these points and he was amazed by how versatile Python is. Whenever I meet someone who asks me where they should start with programming, I recommend they start with Python.

Data analysis is a multistage process. Python supports exceptional methods and procedures in every stage of the data analysis process. There are external libraries that further extend the capabilities of Python for a specific application. It makes Python well-suited for data analysis as well as many other general applications.

1. Python Variables

If you plan to write complex code, then you must include data that will change the execution of the program.

That is what you are going to learn in this chapter. At the end of the chapter, you will learn how the abstract object term can explain each section of data in Python and you will learn how to change objects with the help of variables.

Variables in Python programming are the data types in Python as the name implies. In the programming world, variables are memory location where you store a value. The value that you store might change in the future depending on the descriptions.

In Python, a variable is created once a value is assigned to it. It doesn't need any extra commands to declare a variable in Python. There are specific rules and guidelines to adhere while writing a variable.

Assignment of Variable

Look at variables as a name linked to a specific object. In Python programming, you don't need to declare variables before you use like it is in other programming languages. Instead, you assign a value to a variable and begin to use it immediately. The assignment occurs using a single equals sign (=):

Y= 100

The same way a literal value can be shown from the interpreter using a REPL session, so it is to a variable:

Later if you assign a new value to Y and use it again, the new value is replaced.

Still, Python has room for chained assignment. In other words, you can assign the same value to different variables at the same time.

Example:

This chained assignment allocates 300 to the three variables simultaneously. Most variables in other programming languages are statically typed. This means that a variable is always declared to hold a given data type. Now any value that is assigned to this variable should be similar to the data type of the variable.

However, variables in Python don't follow this pattern. In fact, a variable can hold a value featuring a different data type and later re-assigned to hold another type.

Object References

What really happens when you assign a variable?

This is a vital question in Python programming because it is different from what goes on in other languages.

First, Python is an object-oriented language. In fact, each data item in Python is an object of a given type.

Consider the following example:

When the interpreter comes across the statement print (300), the following takes place:

- Assigns it the value 300.

- Builds an integer object.

- Outputs it to the console.

Python variables are the symbolic name that can act as a pointer to an object. When an object is allocated a variable, a reference to the object can be done using a name. However, the data itself is contained within the object.

The life of an object starts once it is created; at this point, the object may have one reference. In the lifetime of an object, other references to the object can be created. An object will remain active as long as it has one reference.

But when the number of references to the object drops to zero, it cannot be accessed again. The lifetime of the object is then said to be over. Python will finally realize that it is inaccessible and take the allocated space so that it can be used for something different. This process is called garbage collection.

Object Identity

Every object created in Python is assigned a number to identify it. In other words, there is no point where two objects will share the same identifier during a time when the lifetimes of the object overlap. When the count of an object reference drops to zero and it is garbage collected, then the identifying number of the object is reclaimed to be used again.

```
>>> n = 300
>>> m = n
>>> id(n)
60127840
>>> id(m)
60127840

>>> m = 400
>>> id(m)
60127872
```

Cache Small Integer Values

From your knowledge of the variable assignment and referencing of variables in Python, you will not be surprised by:

In this code, Python defines the object of integer type using the value 300 and allows m to refer to it. Similarly, n is allocated to an integer object using the value 300 but not with a different object. Let us consider the following:

In this example, both m and n have been separately allocated to integer objects holding the value 30. But in this instance, id (m) and id (n) are similar.

The interpreter will develop objects between [-5, 256] at the start, and later reuse it. Therefore, if you assign unique variables to an integer value, it will point to the same object.

Variable Names

The previous examples have used short variables like m and n. But still, you can create variable names with long words. This really helps to explain the use of the variable when a user sees the variable.

In general, Python variable names can be of any length and can have upper case and lowercase letters. Also, the variable names can include digits from 0-9 and the underscore character. Another restriction is that the first character of a variable cannot be an integer.

For instance, all these are important variable names:

Since a variable cannot start with a digit, this program will show the following result:

Keep in mind too that lowercase letters and uppercase letters are different. Using the underscore character is important as well:

Nothing will prevent you from defining two variables in the same program that have names like number and Number. However, this is not advised at all. It would definitely confuse anyone going through your code, and even yourself, after you have stayed for a while without looking at the code.

It is important to assign descriptive variable names to make it clear on what it is being used for. For instance, say you are determining the number of people who have graduated from college. You may choose any of the following:

All are great choices than n , or any other variable. At least you can understand from the name the value of the variable.

Reserved Keywords

There is one limit on identifiers names. The Python language has a unique set of keyword that defines specific language functionality. No object can use the same name as a reserved keyword.

Python Keywords

You can see reserved words in python by typing help ("keywords") on the Python interpreter. Reserved keywords are case-sensitive. So you should never change them but use them exactly as they appear. All of them are in lowercase, except for the following:

True, False, and None.

If you attempt to create a variable using a reserved word, it will result in an error.

2. Python Oops Concepts

Python OOPs Concepts

Python object-oriented programming concepts play a vital role in the software industry. It has all the concepts of object-oriented programming. There are many other languages of the same core programming family, but Python is based on OOP concepts from the very beginning. Here, a software expert has the liberty to call functions, objects, and classes to perform any programming task. This language is highly recommended for data science concepts.

- Let's discuss some important parts of OOPs Python:

- Object framework- Quality and methods in Python

- Class- Collection of Objects

- Method- Capacity of an object

- Inheritance- Inherits the qualities of parent object

- Polymorphism- Multiple structures

- Data Abstraction- Central quality of a program

- Encapsulation- Code and data wrapping together

Object framework

This framework has a similar concept in programming as in real world. Any existing substance with some quality is an object. In Python, there is an everywhere object-oriented approach, and all these objects have some specific qualities and functions. Having some defined capacity, objects contain all the important information that is being used to make a comprehensive result-oriented information out of it.

Class- Group of Objects

Class is about the group of objects. These classes have elements with specific attributes. Like in real life, we define classes in programming world as well. For example, we can have a class of students, workers, officers, etc. All classes have some kind of similar traits within the class.

Syntax for Class

class Name of Class:

<statement-1>

<statement-2>

<statement-N>

Method- Capacity of an Object

Method is about the capacity of an object defined in a program. It is based on how many methods an object can have. It is frequently used in Python programming.

Inheritance- Inheriting the quality of parent Object

It is an integral part of Python programming language. In OOP, it is similar to the traditional inheritance system in human biological existence. The younger object has all the traits and methods. Through this framework, we can develop classes to use the properties of one another. It helps in getting results by using single code for every class. It also saves time and can simplify the syntax.

Polymorphism- Multiple structures

This framework is an amazing feature of object-oriented programming. It has similar meaning to its name: multiple structures. It means one assignment is completed in many different methods.

Data Abstraction- Central quality of a program

This framework has excellent features through which it gets precise information to use to execute the functionality. There is no need to run a whole program to achieve results. It takes internal commands and run functionalities. We can tag functions with some names and can call them to get the functionality.

Encapsulation- Code and data wrapping together

Encapsulated code and data are an essential part of programming. It restricts the approach and code within specified users. It is done intentionally for using it in combination and keeping it secure.

Object-oriented versus Procedure-oriented Programming languages

Object-oriented	Procedural Programming
Object-oriented programming is the critical thinking approach and utilized where calculation is finished by using objects.	Procedural programming utilizes a rundown of instructions to do calculation bit by bit.

It makes the improvement and maintenance easier.	In procedural programming, It isn't difficult to maintain the codes when the undertaking ends up extensive.
It mimics this present reality element. So true issues can be effectively settled through oops.	It doesn't reenact this present reality. It chips away at bit by bit; instructions separated into little parts called capacities.
It gives data hiding. Therefore, it is more secure than procedural dialects. You can't access to private data from anywhere.	Procedural language doesn't give any legitimate method to data binding, so it is less secure.
Example of object-oriented programming	Example of procedural dialects are: C, Fortran, Pascal, VB, and so on.

dialects is C++, Java, .Net, Python, C#, etc.	

Python Class and Objects

A class is basically an assumed element that contains number of objects. It is virtual and gives meaning to us when we look at it with reference to objects and their properties. For example, assume a hospital building. It has rooms, beds, medical equipment, and so on. The hospital building is a class, and all the parts of the building are its objects.

In this area of the instructional exercise, we will talk about creating classes and objects in Python. We will also discuss how to get to a characteristic by using the class object.

Creating classes in Python

Python has a very simple syntax for crating classes. A non-technical individual can make a class by just typing simple commands.

Syntax

 class ClassName:

#statement_suite

Consider the following guide to make a class Employee, which contains two fields as Employee id, and name.

The class likewise contains a capacity show() which is utilized to show the information of the Employee.

Example:

```
class Employee:
id = 10;
name = "ayush"
def display (self):
print(self.id,self.name)
```

Here, self is utilized as a source of a perspective variable which alludes to the present class object. It is consistently the main argument in the capacity definition. Be that as it may, using self is discretionary in the capacity call.

Creating an instance of the class

A class should be instantiated on the off chance that we need to utilize the class characteristics in another class.

It can be instantiated by calling the class using the class name.

Example:

```
id number = 10;
name = "John"
print("ID number: %d \nName: %s"%(self.id,self.name))
emp = Employee()
emp.display()
```

Output:

ID number: 10

      Name: John

Python Constructor

It is a special type of method (function) that is used to initialize the specified members in a class.

There are two types of Constructors:

- Parameterized Constructor
- Non-parameterized Constructor

Its definition is executed when we create the object of this class. Constructors verify that there are measurable resources for the object to perform a task for start-up.

Creating the constructor in Python

In Python, the method __init__ generated the constructor of the class. This method is used when the class is instantiated. We can pass a number of arguments at the time of making the class object, using __init__ definition. Every class should have a constructor, even if it is simply the default constructor.

Example:

```
class Student:
count = 0
def __init__(self):
Student.count = Student.count + 1
s1=Student()
s2=Student()
s3=Student()
print("The number of students:",Student.count)
```

Output:

The number of students: 3

Python Non-Parameterized Constructor Example:

```python
class Student:

    def __init__(my):
        print("It is non parametrized constructor")
    def show(my,name):
        print("Hello",name)
y = Student()
y.show("Jack")
```

Output:

It is non parametrized constructor
Hello Jack

Parameterized Constructor Example:

```python
    def __init__(my, firstname):
        print(" parametrized constructor")
```

```
my.firstname = name
def show(my):
print("Hello",my.firstname)
s = Student("Jack")

s.show()
```

Output:

parametrized constructor

Hello Jack

Python In-built class functions

Python has multiple in-built class functions. Let's try to understand its functionality through an example.

Example:

```
class Workers:
def __init__(my,name,age):
my.name = name;
my.age = age
W = worker("Jack",115,22)
print(getattr(W,'name'))
setattr(W,"age",24)
print(getattr(s,'age'))
```

```
delattr(s,'age')
print(s.age)
```

Output:

Jack

24

True

AttributeError: There is no attribute 'age' in Student' object.

Built-in class attributes

A class in Python also contains class attributes (built-in) which give information about the class.

Here is the list of built-in class attributes:

Attribute Description

__dict__

It is for providing the dictionary containing the information about the class namespace.

__doc__

It is to contain a string that has the class documentation.

__name__

It accesses the class name.

__module__

It accesses the module in which, this class is defined.

__bases__

It is to have a tuple.

Example:

```python
def __init__(my,name,roll number,age):
my.name = name;
my.rollbumber = roll number;
m.age = age
def display_details(my):
print("Name:%s, Roll Number:%d,
age:%d"%(my.name,my.roll number))
Y = Student("Jack",10,17)
print(y.__doc__)
print(y.__dict__)
print(y.__module_)
```

Output:

None

{'name': 'Jack', 'Roll number': 10, 'age': 17}

___main___

Python Inheritance

Python inheritance is a very unique feature of the programming language. It improves the usability of the program and development. In this framework, a child class can access the qualities and functionalities of parent class.

Syntax

class derived-class(base class):

<class-suite>

Consider the following syntax.

Syntax

class derive-class(<base class 1>, <base class 2>, ...
<base class n>):

<class - suite>

Example:

```
class Animal:
def speak(self):
print("Animal Speaking")
#child class Dog inherits the base class Animal
class Dog(Animal):
def bark(self):
print("barking dog")
d = Dog()
d.bark()
d.speak()
```

Output:

barking dog
Animal Speaking

Python Multi-Level inheritance

This inheritance has multiple levels in Python. Similarly, it has in other programming languages. This object-oriented feature is very useful to derive data from one class and to us it in another.

The syntax of multi-level inheritance:

Syntax:

```
class class1:
<class-suite>
class class2(class1):
<class suite>
class class3(class2):
<class suite>
```

Example:

```
class Animal:
 def speak(self):
print("Speaking Animal")
  #The child class Dog inherits the base class Animal
class Dog(Animal):
def bark(self):
print("barking dog")
#The child class Dogchild inherits another child class Dog
class DogChild(Dog):
def eat(self):
print("Bread eating...")
d = DogChild()
d.bark()
d.speak()
```

d.eat()

Output:

barking dog
Speaking Animal
Bread eating...

Python Multiple inheritance

Python gives the possibility to inherit multiple base classes in the child class.

Syntax

class Base1:
<class-suite>
class Base2:
<class-suite>
class BaseN:
<class-suite>

Example:

class Calculate1:
def Summation(self,a,b):

```python
return a+b;
class Calculate2:
def Multiplication(self,a,b):
return a*b;
class Derive(Calculate1,Calculate2):
def Divide(self,a,b):
return a/b;
d = Derive()
print(isinstance(d,Derive))
```

Output:

True

Method Overriding

We can give specific implementation of the parent class method in our child class. Using or defining parent class method on a child class is called method over-riding.

Example:

```python
class Bank:
def getroi(self):
return 10;
class SBI(Bank):
```

```python
def getroi(self):
return 7;
class ICICI(Bank):
def getroi(self):
return 8;
a1 = Bank()
a2 = SBI()
a3 = ICICI()
print("Bank interest:",a1.getroi());
print("SBI interest:",a2.getroi());
print("ICICI interest:",a3.getroi());
```

Output:

Bank interest: 10

SBI interest: 7

ICICI interest: 8

Data abstraction in Python

Abstraction is a significant part of object-oriented programming. In Python, we can likewise perform data hiding by adding the twofold underscore (____) as a prefix to the credit that is to be covered up. After this, the property won't be noticeable outside of the class through the object.

Example:

```
class Employee:
count = 0;
def __init__(self):
Employee.__count = Employee.__count+1
def display(self):
print("The number of employees",Employee.__count)
emp = Employee()
emp2 = Employee()
try:
print(emp.__count)
finally:
1emp.display()
```

Output:

The number of employees 2

AttributeError: 'Employee' object has no attribute '__count'

3. Python Magic Method

Python magic method is defined as the uncommon method that includes "magic" to a class. It starts and finishes with twofold underscores, for instance, _init_ or _str_.

The built-in classes define numerous magic methods. The dir() capacity can be utilized to see the quantity of magic methods inherited by a class. It has two prefixes, and addition underscores in the method name.

It is mostly used to define the over-burden practices of predefined administrators.

___init___

The _init_ method is called after the making of the class; however, before it came back to the guest. It is invoked with no call, when an instance of the class is made like constructors in other programming dialects. For example, C++, Java, C#, PHP, and so forth. These methods are otherwise called initialize and are called after _new_. Its where you ought to initialize the instance factors.

___str___

This capacity processes "informal" or a pleasantly printable string portrayal of an object and should restore a string object.

__repr__

This capacity is called by the repr() built-in capacity to figure the "official" string portrayal of an object and returns a machine-discernible portrayal of a kind. The objective of the _repr_ is to be unambiguous.

__len__

This capacity should restore the object's length.

__call__

An object is made callable by adding the _call_ magic method, and it is another method that isn't required as frequently is _call_.

Whenever defined in a class, at that point that class can be called. In any case, in the event that it was a capacity instance itself instead of modifying.

__del__

Similarly, _init_ is a constructor method, _del_ and resembles a destructor. In the event that you have opened a document in _init _, at that point _del_ can close it.

__bytes__

It offers to figure a byte-string portrayal of an object and should restore a string object.

__ge__

This method gets invoked when >= administrator is utilized and returns True or False.

__neg__

This capacity gets required the unary administrator.

__ipow__

This capacity gets approached the types with arguments. For example, a**=b.

__le__

This capacity gets approached correlation using <= administrator.

__nonzero__

Python Stack and Queue

Python stacks and queue are the most basic functions. They are used to access the data to and to alter it for some purpose. These data structures are famous in computer software world. Queues have a rule FIFO (First In First Out) for sorting data, while stack follows LIFO (Last In First Out) method.

Stack Attributes:

push - It adds a component to the highest point of the stack.

pop - It expels a component from the highest point of the stack.

Tasks on Stack:

Addition – It increases the size of stack.

Cancellation – It is used to decrease the size of stack.

Traversing - It involves visiting every component of the stack.

Qualities:

- Insertion request of the stack is saved.
- Helpful for parsing the activities.
- Duplicacy is permitted.

Code

Code to demonstrate Implementation of

stack using list

```
y= ["Python-language", "Csharp", "Androidnew"]

y.push("Javaflash")

y.push("C++lang")

print(y)

print(y.pop())

print(y)

print(y.pop())

print(y)
```

Output:

```
['Python-language', 'Csharp', 'Androidnew', 'Javaflash',
'C++lang']

C++lang

['Python-language', 'Csharp', 'Androidnew', 'Javaflash']

Javaflash

['Python-language', 'Csharp', 'Androidnew']
```

Queue Attributes

First-in-First-Out (FIFO) principle allows queue to have elements from both ends. It is open to get in and let go of components.

Basic functionalities in queue:

enqueue – For adding elements.

dequeue – For removing elements from queue.

Qualities

- Insertion request of the queue is protected.
- Duplicacy is permitted.
- Valuable for parsing CPU task activities.

Code

```
import queue
# Queue is created as an object 'L'
L = queue.Queue(maxsize=10)
# Data is inserted in 'L' at the end using put()
L.put(9)
L.put(6)
L.put(7)
L.put(4)
# get() takes data from
# from the head
# of the Queue
```

```
print(L.get())
print(L.get())
print(L.get())
print(L.get())
```

Output:

9

6

7

4

Command line arguments in Python

Python focuses to provide command lines for input parameters that are passed to elements in order to execute functions.

By using getopt module, this operation is executed.

The getopt module of Python

It is very similar to other programming languages. It is used to pass inputs through command lines to get options from the user. It allows a user to input options.

Python Assert Keyword

These keywords inform the programmer about the realities of running the program. It works with conditional commands. When the condition doesn't get fulfilled, it declines with the display of an assertive message on the screen e.g. "no data is available". AssertionErrors are used to define the program properly.

Why Assertion?

It is a highly recommended debugging tool. It keeps the user aware about codes on each step. If some lines of codes have errors or mistakes, it alerts the user with message.

Syntax

assert condition, error_message(optional)

Example:

def avg(scores):

assert len(scores) != 0,"The List is empty."

return sum(scores)/len(scores)

scoresb = [67,59,86,75,92]

print("The Average of scoresb:",avg(scoresb))

scores1 = []

print("The Average of scoresa:",avg(scoresa))

Output:

The Average of scores2: 75.8
AssertionError: The List is empty.

Python Modules, Exceptions and Arrays

Python modules, exceptions and arrays are an integral part of object-oriented Python programming language. In data science, we use them from time to time to have a better understanding with the usage of code in a logical way. These programming methods are also used in other programming languages, and are a popular framework because of their usage to transform the complexities of programming into simple coding. Let's discuss them one by one.

Python Modules

Python modules are programs that have programming codes in Python. They contain all variables, classes and functions of this unique language. They enable the programmer to organize codes in a proper format that is logically valid. They can be imported to use the functionality of one module for another.

Example:

Now here a module named as file.py will be generated which contains a function func that has a code to print some message on the console.

So let's generate it *file.py.*

#displayMsg prints a message to the name.

def displayMsg(name)

print("Hi "+name);

Now it is required to add this module into the main module to call the method displayMsg() defined in the module named file.

Loading the module in our Python code

In order to utilize the functionality of Python code, the module is loaded. Python provides two types of statements as defined below.

1. The import statement

2. The from-import statement

Python Standard Library- Built-in Modules

There is an unlimited pool of Python Built-in Modules. We will discuss some of the most important modules. These are:

- **random**
- **statistics**
- **math**
- **datetime**
- **csv**

To import any of them, use this syntax:

Import[module_name]

eg. Import random

Random module in Python

This module is used to generate numbers. By using the command random(), we can generate float numbers. The range of these float numbers lies between 0.0 and 1.0.

Here are some important random functions used in random module:

The Function random.randint()

It is for random integers.

The Function random.randrange()

It is for randomly selected elements.

The Function random.choice()

It is for randomly selected elements from non-empty.

The Statistics module of Python

It is a very useful module of Python. It provides numerical data after performing statistics functions.

Here is a list of some very commonly used functions of this module:

The mean() function

It performs arithmetic mean of the list.

For Example:

import statistics

datalist = [5, 2, 7, 4, 2, 6, 8]

a= statistics.mean(datalist)

print("The Mean will be:", a)

Output:

The Mean will be: 4.857142857142857

The median() function

It gives middle value of the list.

Example:

import statistics

dataset = [4, -5, 6, 6, 9, 4, 5, -2]

print("Median of data-set is : % s "

% (statistics.median(dataset)))

Median of data-set is: 4.5

The mode() function

It provides common data from the list.

Example:

import statistics

datasets =[2, 4, 7, 7, 2, 2, 3, 6, 6, 8]

print("Calculated Mode % s" %
(statistics.mode(datasets)))

Output:

Calculated Mode 2

The stdev() function

It calculates the standard deviation.

Example:

import statistics

sample = [7, 8, 9, 10, 11]

print("Standard Deviations of sample data is % s "

% (statistics.stdev(sample)))

Output:

Standard Deviation of sample data is
1.5811388300841898

The median_low()

The median_low function is used to return the low
median of numeric data in the list.

Example:

import statistics

simple list of a set of integers

set1 = [4, 6, 2, 5, 7, 7]

Print low median of the data-set

print ("data-set Low median is % s "

% (statistics.median_low(set1)))

Output:

Low median of the data-set is 5

median_high()

The median_high () function is employed to calculate the high median of numeric data in the list.

Example:

import statistics

list of set of the integers

dataset = [2, 1, 7, 6, 1, 9]

print("High median of data-set is %s "

 % (statistics.median_high(dataset)))

Output:

High median of the data-set is 6

The math module of Python

This module contains the mathematical functions to perform every mathematical calculation.

Here are two constants as well:

Pie (n): A well-known mathematical constant and is defined as the ratio of circumstance to the diameter of a circle. Its value is 3.141592653589793.

Euler's number (e): It is the base of the natural logarithmic, and its value is 2.718281828459045.

A few math modules which are given below:

The math.log10() function

It calculates base1 0 logarithm of the number.

Example:

*im*port math

x=13 # small value of of x

print('log10(x) is :', math.log10(x))

Output:

log10(x) is : 1.1139433523068367

The math.sqrt() function

It calculates the root of the number.

Example:

import math

x = 20

y = 14

z = 17.8995

```
print('sqrt of 20 is ', math.sqrt(x))

print('sqrt of 14 is ', math.sqrt(y))

print('sqrt of 17.8995 is ', math.sqrt(z))
```

Output:

sqrt of 20 is 4.47213595499958

 sqrt of 14 is 3.7416573867739413

 sqrt of 17.8995 is 4.230780069916185

The math.expm1() function

This method calculates e raised to the power of any number minus 1. e is the base of natural logarithm.

The math.cos() function

It calculates cosine of any number in radians.

Example:

```
import math

angleInDegree = 60

angleInRadian = math.radians(angleInDegree)

print('Given angle :', angleInRadian)
```

```
print('cos(x) is :', math.cos(angleInRadian))
```

Output:

Given angle : 1.0471975511965976

cos(x) is : 0.5000000000000001

The math.sin() function

It calculates the sine of any number, in radians.

Example:

```
import math
angleInDegree = 60
angleInRadian = math.radians(angleInDegree)
print('Given angle :', angleInRadian)
print('sin(x) is :', math.sin(angleInRadian))
```

Output:

Given angle: 1.0471975511965976

sin(x) is: 0.8660254037844386

The math.tan() function

It returns the tangent of any number, in radians.

Example:

import math

angleInDegree = 60

angleInRadian = math.radians(angleInDegree)

print('Given angle :', angleInRadian)

print('tan(x) is :', math.tan(angleInRadian))

Output:

Given angle : 1.0471975511965976

 tan(x) is : 1.7320508075688767

The sys module of Python

This module provides access to system-specific functions. It changes the Python Runtime Environment to enable the user to get variables and parameters.

Need to import sys function

First, there is a need to import the sys module in the program before starting the use of functions.

The sys.modules' function

These functions perform some really important tasks on system in Python programming.

- Function of sys.argv: *For arguments*
- Function of sys.base_prefix: *For startup*
- Function of sys.byteorder*: To get byterorder.*
- *Function of sys.maxsize*: To get large integer.
- Function of sys.path*: To set path.*
- Function of sys.stdin*: To restore files.*
- *Function of sys.getrefcount*: To get reference count of an object.
- *Fun tion of sys.exit*: To exit from Python command prompt.
- *Function of sys executable*: Locate the Python in system.
- *sys.platform:* To identify Platform.

The Collection Module of Python

This module plays an important role, as it collects major data formats or data structures, such as list, dictionary, set, and tuple. It improves the functionality of the current version of Python. It is defined as a container that is employed to conserve collections of data, for example, list.

The function of namedtuple() in Collection Module

It produces a tuple object without causing an issue with indexing.

Examples:

John = ('John', 25, 'Male')

print(John)

Output:

('John', 25, 'Male')

OrderedDict() function

It generates dictionary object with key that can overwrite data inside.

Example:

```
import collections

d1=collections.OrderedDict()

d1['A']=15

d1['C']=20

d1['B']=25

d1['D']=30

for k,v in d1.items():

print (k,v)
```

Output:

```
A 15

 C 20

 B 25

 D 30
```

Function defaultdict()

It produces an object similar to dictionary.

Example:

```
from collections import defaultdict

number = defaultdict(int)

number['one'] = 1

number['two'] = 2

print(number['three'])
```

Output:

0

Counter() function

It counts the hasbale objects after reviewing the elements of list.

Example:

```
A = Counter()

Xlist = [1,2,3,4,5,7,8,5,9,6,10]

Counter(Xlist)

Counter({1:5,2:4})

Ylist = [1,2,4,7,5,1,6,7,6,9,1]

c = Counter(Ylist)

print(A[1])
```

Result:

3

The function deque()

It facilitates addition and removal of elements from both ends.

For Example:

```
from collections import deque

list = ["x","y","z"]

deq = deque(list)

print(deq)
```

Output:

deque(['x', 'y', 'z'])

Python OS Module

Python OS module provides functions utilized for interacting with the operating system and also obtains related data about it. The OS comes under Python's standard utility modulesPython OS module which allows you to work with the files, documents and directories. Some of OS module functions are as follows:

os.name

It provides the name of the operating system module it imports.

It can register 'posix', 'nt', 'os2', 'ce', 'java' and 'riscos'.

Example:

import os

print(os.name)

Output:

posix

os.getcwd()

It restores the Current Working Directory (CWD) of the file.

Example:

import os

print(os.getcwd())

Output:

C:\Users\Python\Desktop\ModuleOS

os.error

The functions in this module define the OS level errors in case of invalid file names and path.

Example:

import os

filename1 = 'PythonData.txt'

 f = open(filename1, 'rU')

 text = f.read()

 f.close()

print('Difficult read: ' + filename1)

Output:

Difficult read: PythonData.txt

os.popen()

It opens a file, and it gives back a fileobject that contains connection with pipe.

The datetime Module

It is an imported module that allows you to create date and time objects. It works to conduct many functions related to date and time.

Let's understand it through an example:

Example:

import datetime;

#returns the current datetime object

print(datetime.datetime.now())

Output:

2018-12-18 16:16:45.462778

Python read csv file

The Comma Separated values (CSV) File

It is a simple file format that arranges tabular data. It is used to store data in tabular form ora spreadsheet that can be exchanged when needed. It is in a Microsoft excel supported data form.

The CSV Module Functions in Python

This module helps in reading/writing CSV files. It takes the data from columns and stores it to use in the future.

- The function csv.field_size_limit - *To maximize field size.*
- *The function csv.reader –* To read information or data from a csv file.
- *The function csv.writer –* To write the information or data to a csv file

   These functions have a major role in CSV module.

The Exceptions in Python

Exceptions are actually interruptions that stops the running program. They are mistakes or errors in the code. In Python, these are handled differently.

The Common Exceptions in Python

Here are some common exceptions that may occur in Python. Every Python programmer is very familiar with these errors or exceptions.

- *The exception of ZeroDivisionError:* when a number is divided by zero.
- *The exception of NameError:* when a name is not found.
- *The exception of IndentationError:* when incorrect indentation is given.
- *The exception of IOError:* when Input Output operation fails.
- *The exception of EOFError:* when the end of the file is reached, and still operations are being performed.

Unhandled Exceptions

Example:

```
x= int(input("Enter a:"))

y = int(input("Enter b:"))

z= a/b;

print("x/y = %d"%c)

print("Hello I am a teacher")
```

Output:

Enter a:10

Enter b:0

Traceback (most recent call last):

File "exception-test.py", line 3, in <module>

  c = a/b;

ZeroDivisionError: division by zero

The finally block

It is used to run a code before the try statement.

Syntax

try:

block of code

this may throw an exception

finally:

block of code

this will always be executed

Example:

try:

fileptr = open("file.txt","r")

```
try:

fileptr.write("Hi I am good")

finally:

fileptr.close()

print("file closed")

except:

print("Error")
```

Output:

file closed

Error

The Exception Raising in Python

The raise clause in Python is used to raise an exception.

Syntax

Raise exception_class,<value>

The Custom Exception in Python

It enables programmers to generate exceptions that have already been launched with the program.

Example:

```python
class ErrorInCode(Exception):

def __init__(self, data):

self.data = data

def __str__(self):

return repr(self.data)

try:

raise ErrorInCode(2000)

except ErrorInCode as ae:

print("Received error:", ae.data)
```

Output:

> *Received error: 2000*

Python Arrays

Array is a set of elements that are used to work on specific data values. It is advanced level programming that allows users multiple functionality over data structures. Through arrays, code can be simplified, therefore saving a lot of time.

Array Element - Data element stored in array.

Array Index - Position of an element.

Array Representation:

The declaration of array can be done in many different ways.

- Array Index starts with 0.
- Element can be located with the help of its index number.
- The length of the array defines the storage capacity of the elements.

Array operations in Python:

Some of the basic operations in an array are given below:

- *Traverse* – To print all the elements one by one.
- *Insertion* – Addition of element in Index.
- *Deletion* – Deletion of element at index.

- **Search** – *To search the element.*

  - *Update* - To update an element at the given index.

Array Generation

array *import* *

MyarrayName = array(typecode, [initializers])

Accessing array elements

The array elements accessibility can be ensured by using the respective indices of those elements.

import array as arr

a = arr.array('i', [1, 3, 5, 87])

print("First element:", a[0])

print("Second element:", a[1])

print("Second last element:", a[-1])

Output:

First element: 1

Second element: 3

Second last element: 8

Arrays are changeable, and elements can be changed in similar to lists.

A combination of arrays makes the process speedy and saves time. The array can reduce the code's size.

Deletion can be done by using the *del* statement in Python.

The length of an array can be described as the number of elements in an array. It returns an integer value that is equal to the total number of the elements present in that array.

Syntax

len(array_name)

Example:

a=arr.array('d',[1.2 , 2.2 ,3.2,3,6,7.8])

b=arr.array('d',[4.5,8.6])

c=arr.array('d')

c=a+b

print("Array c = ",c)

Output:

Array c= array('d', [1.2, 2.2, 3.2, 3.6, 7.8, 4.5, 8.6])

Example:

import array as arr

x = arr.array('i', [5, 10, 15, 20])

print("First element:", x[0])

print("Second element:", x[1])

print("Second last element:", x[-1])

Output:

First element: 5

Second element: 10

Second last element: 15

4. The Principles Of Algorithm Design

Algorithms are all-important; they are the very foundation of computers and computer science. Your computer may be constructed of hardware items, but without algorithms, it's all a waste of space. The Turing Machine is the theoretical foundation of all algorithms and this was established many years before we even thought about implementing a machine like that using digital logic circuits. The Turing Machine is a model that can translate a set of given inputs into outputs, working to a set of pre-defined rules, much like today's Machine Learning.

Algorithms affect our lives in more ways than we realize. Take page ranking on search engines for example. These are based on algorithms and these allow anyone to search quickly through huge amounts of information. This, in turn, hastens the rate at which new research can be done, new discoveries can be found, and with which innovative technologies can be developed.

Studying algorithms is also essential because it makes us think about problems in specific ways. Our mental abilities sharpen, and we can improve our problem-solving abilities by learning to find and isolate the core components of a problem and define the relationship between them.

In its simplest form, an algorithm is nothing more than a list of instructions to be carried out in sequence. Think of it, in Python terms, as a linear form of do x, then do y, and then do z. However, we can change things and make these algorithms do more by adding if-else statements. By doing that, the direction the action takes then depends on conditions being met, and then we add operations, while statements, for statements, and iteration. To expand our algorithm a bit more, we add recursion which often provides the same result that iteration does even though they are very different. Recursive functions apply the function to inputs that get progressively smaller. The input of one recursive step is the output of the previous one.

Paradigms of Algorithm Design

There are three main paradigms to algorithm design:

- Divide and Conquer
- Greedy
- Dynamic programming

Let's take these one at a time. Divide and conquer is self-explanatory – the problem is broken down into small subproblems and the results of each one combined into an overall solution. This has to be one of the most common techniques to solve problems and is perhaps the most common approach to the design of algorithms.

Greedy algorithms involve optimizing and combining. In short, it means to take the shortest path to the most useful solution for local problems, all the while hoping that somewhere it will all lead to the global solution.

Dynamic programming is most useful when the subproblems start to overlap. This is not the same as the divide and conquers paradigm. Instead of breaking the problem down into individual subproblems, intermediate solutions get cached and then used in a later operation. It does use recursion like divide and conquers but, with dynamic programming, we compare the results at different times. This provides a boost in terms of performance for some types of problems; it can be quicker to retrieve a previous result than it is to go through recalculating it.

Backtracking and Recursion

Recursion is incredibly useful in terms of divide and conquer but it can be hard to see exactly what is going on; each of the recursive calls spins off another recursive call. There are two types of cases at the heart of a recursive function:

- Base case – this tells recursion when it should terminate
- Recursive case – this calls the function the case is in

The calculation of factorials is one of the simplest examples of a problem that results in a recursive solution. The factorial algorithm is responsible for defining 2 cases:

- The base case where n is equal to zero
- The recursive case where n is more than zero. Here is an example of implementation:

When this code is printed, we get 1, 2, 6, 24. For 24 to be calculated, we need the parent call and four recursive calls. On each of the recursions, a copy is made of the method variables and it is stored in memory. When the method has returned, that copy is removed.

It isn't always going to be clear whether iteration or recursion is the best result for a problem. Both repeat sets of operations and both work well with divide and conquer. Iteration keeps on going until the problem has been solved and recursion breaks it down into ever smaller chunks combining the results from each one. Iteration does tend to be better for programmers because control tends to remain local to the loop; with recursion, you get a closer representation to factorials and other like mathematical concepts. Recursive calls are stored in the memory; iterations aren't. All of this leads to trade-offs between memory use and processor cycles, so determination may come down to whether your task is memory or processor intensive.

Backtracking

Backtracking is a type of recursion that tends to be used more for problems like the traversal of tree structures. In these problems, each node presents us with several options and we need to choose one of them. Doing that leads to more options; dependent on the options chosen throughout, we either reach a dead end or a goal state. If the former, we need to backtrack to an earlier node and go down a different route. Backtracking is also a kind of divide and conquers method when we need to do exhaustive searches. More importantly, when we backtrack, we prune off the branches that don't provide any results. Look at this example of backtracking; a recursive approach has been used to generate all the permutations that are possible for a given strength of a given length:

Notice that we have two recursive calls and a 'double list' compression. This results in all the elements of the first sequence being concatenated recursively with the return when n=1. Each of the string elements was generated in the recursive call that came before.

Divide and Conquer - Long Multiplication

Recursion isn't just a clever little trick, but to understand what it can do, we need to compare it to approaches like iteration and we need to be able to understand when to use it for a faster algorithm. In primary math, we all learned an iterative algorithm used for the multiplication of a pair of large numbers. That algorithm was long multiplication involving iterative multiplication and carrying, followed by shifting and addition.

What we want to do is work out whether this procedure really is all that efficient for the multiplication of the numbers. When you multiply two numbers each four digits long, it takes no less than 16 multiplication operations. This method of algorithm analysis, in terms of how many computational primitives are needed, is vital because it provides us with a way of understanding what the relationship is between the time taken to do the computation and the input size to the computation. What we really want to know is, what will happen when the input is massive? We call this topic asymptomatic analysis, otherwise known as time complexity, and it is important when studying algorithms; we will talk about it quite a bit through the course of this section of the book.

A Recursive Approach

As far as long multiplication goes, there is a better way; several algorithms exist for the more efficient operation of multiplying large numbers. The Karatsuba algorithm is one of the best-known long multiplication alternatives and it dates back to 1962. This algorithm takes a very different approach instead of iterative multiplication of single digits, it does recursive multiplication on inputs that progressively get smaller. A recursive program will call itself on each small subset of the parent input.

To build an algorithm, we need to take a large number and decompose it into smaller numbers. The easiest way is to split it into two – one half with important digits and one with less important digits. For example, a number with 4 digits of 2345 would become 2 sets of numbers, each with 2 digits, 23 and 45.

Let's take 2 n digit numbers and write a general decomposition for them. The numbers are x and y and m is a positive integer with a lower value than n:

This does suggest that we are using recursion to multiply the numbers because the process involves multiplication. More specifically, ac, ad, bc, and bd all have smaller numbers than the input making it not inconceivable that the same operation could be applied as a partial solution to the bigger problem. So far, the algorithm has four recursive steps (all multiplication) and it is not yet clear whether this would be more efficient than traditional long multiplication.

So far, we have looked at nothing more than what mathematicians have known for years. However, the Karatsuba algorithm goes a step further and observes that we only really need to know three of the quantities to solve the equation. Those quantities are $z_2 = ac$; $z_1 = ad + bc$ and $z_0 = bd$. We only need to know what the values of a, b, c, and d, are in as much as they contribute to the overall sum and the products required to calculate z_2, z_1, and z_0. This brings about the possibility that we could reduce how many recursive steps are needed and, as it turns out, we can do that.

Because ac and bd have already been reduced to their simplest form, we can't really take these calculations out. What we can do is this:

(a+b)(c+d)=ac+bd+ad+bc

When ac and bd, calculated previously, are taken away, we are left with the quantity that we need – (ad + bc):

ac+bd+ad+bc-ac-bc=ad+bc

What this shows is that it is perfectly possible to compute ad+bc without having to compute the individual quantities separately.

Below is the Karatsuba algorithm in a Python implementation:

```
from math import log10, ceil

def karatsuba(x,y):
    # The base case for recursion
    #sets n, which is the number of digits in the highest
input number
    #adds 1 if n is uneven
    n = n if n % 2 == 0 else n + 1
    #splits the input numbers
    #applies the three recursive steps
    #performs the multiplication
```

```
    return (((10**n)*ac) + bd +
 ((10**n_2)*(ad_bc)))
```

Just to satisfy ourselves that this really works, there is a test function we can run:

Runtime Analysis

By now, it should be clear that one of the more important sides of algorithm design is gauging how efficient it is in terms of time, or how many operations, and memory. The analysis of the number of operations is called Runtime Analysis. There are several ways to run this and the most obvious is nothing more than a measurement of the time taken for the algorithm to finish. There are problems with this approach; how long it takes depends on what hardware it is run, for a start. Another way, independent of the platform, is to count how many operations it takes, but this also causes problems in that we don't have any definitive way of quantifying operations. This would depend on the programming language used, the style of coding, and how we opt to count the operations. However, we could use this way if we were to combine it with an expectation that the runtime increases as the input size increases and it does it in a specific way. In other words, that there is a relationship mathematically between the input size (n) and the time the algorithm takes to run. There are three principles that guide this, and their importance will become clear as we go on.

First, the principles:

- Making no assumptions about the input data giving us a worst-case analysis
- Ignoring or suppressing lower order terms and constant factors – with larger inputs, the higher-order terms will be dominant
- Focus only on those problems with the large inputs.

The first one is very useful because it provides us with an upper bound that is tight – the algorithm is guaranteed to fail. The second is just about ignoring anything that doesn't contribute majorly to the runtime making work easier and letting us focus on what impacts performance more.

With the Karatsuba algorithm, the square of the input size increased, and so did the number of operations used for multiplication. With a four-digit number, we use 16 operations and with an eight-digit number, we need 64. However, we're not so interested in how an algorithm with small n values behaves so we ignore the factors that only increase linearly or lowly. At the higher n values, the operations that increase fast as n is increased will be the dominant ones.

We'll talk briefly about the merge-sort algorithm here because it is useful to learn about performance at runtime. This is one of the classic algorithms from more than 60 years ago and it is still used today in some of the highly popular sorting libraries. Merge-sort is recursive and uses divide and conquer, which, as you know, means breaking a problem down, sorting the parts recursively, and putting the results together. Merge-sort is an obvious demonstration of this algorithm design paradigm.

Merge-sort has just three steps:

- Sorts the left side of the input array recursively
- Sorts the right side of the input array recursively
- Merges the sorted arrays into one

One typical use is to sort numbers into numerical order. Merge-sort will divide the list in two and work on each side in parallel. Here is the Python code for the algorithm:

The easiest way to determine the running time performance is to start by mapping the recursive calls onto a tree structure with each tree node being a call that works on an ever-smaller subprogram. Each time we invoke merge-sort, we get two recursive calls, so we can use a binary tree to represent this, with each child node getting an input subset. To work out the time the algorithm takes to finish relative to n, we start by working out how much work there is and how many operations are on each tree level.

Keeping our focus on the runtime analysis, on the first level we have two n/2 subproblems; level two gives us four, and so on. So, when does the recursion get to its base case? Simply, when the array is one or zero. To get to a number that is nearly one, we take the number of recursive levels and divide n by 2 that many times. This is the definition of log2 and, as the first recursive level is 0, the number of levels is log2n+1.

Let's refine the definitions. Up to now, we have used n to represent the number of elements in an input, referring to how many elements are in the first recursive level, or the length of the first input. What we need to do is be able to know the difference between the initial input length and the input length at each recursive level. For this, we use m i.e. mj for the input length at recursive level j.

Using recursion trees for algorithm analysis has the advantage of being able to know what is done at each recursive level. Defining the work is the number of operations in relation to the input size. We must measure the performance of an algorithm in a way that is independent of the platform although runtime will depend on the hardware. It is important to count how many operations there are because this is our metric related directly to the performance of our algorithm.

Generally, because we get two recursive calls each time merge-sort is invoked, each level has double the number of calls of the previous one. At the same time, each call is working on an input that is half the size of its parent. To work out how many operations there are, we must know how many operations are used by one merge of two sub-arrays. Look at the Python code above. After the first two recursive calls, we can count the operations – three assignments followed by three while loops. The first loop has an if-else statement and within each is a comparison and an assignment – two operations. This is counted as a set and there is only one set in an if-else, so this set was carried out m times. The last two while loops each have an assignment operation, making for a total of 4m+3 operations for each merge-sort recursion.

Because m has to be at least 1, the number of operations has an upper bound of 7m. This is not an exact science; it all depends on how the operations are counted. We haven't included any increment or housekeeping operations as we are only interested in the runtime growth rate related to n at the high n values.

All this may seem a bit daunting because every call from a recursive call spins off to even more recursive calls and things look as if they exponentially explode. What makes this manageable is as the recursive calls double, the subproblem size halves. These cancel each other out very nicely as we will demonstrate.

To work out the max number of the operations on each tree level, the number of subproblems are multiplied by the number of operations in each of those subproblems, like this:

$2j \times 7(n/2j) = 7n$

What we see here is 2jcancels out how the number of operations there are on each level independently of the level, giving us an upper bound to work with. In our example, it is 7n. This number includes the operations that each recursive call performs on that level only, not on any other. From this, as we get a doubling of the recursive calls for each level, and this is counter-balanced by the subproblem input size halving on each level.

If we wanted to know how many operations there were for one complete merge-sort, we would take the number of operations per level and multiply that by the total number of levels, like this:

$7n(\log 2n + 1)$

Expanding that gives us:

$7n \log 2n + 7$

The key to take from this is that the relationship between input size and running time has a logarithmic component and, if you remember your high-school math, logarithm functions flatten off fast. As x, an input variable, increases in size, so y, the output variable, will increase by progressively smaller amounts.

Asymptotic Analysis

Runtime performance of an algorithm can be characterized in one of three ways:

- Worst-case – using an input that is slow to perform
- Best case – using an input that gives us the best results
- Average case – assuming the input is random

To calculate each one, we must know what the lower and upper bounds are. We looked at using mathematical expressions to represent runtime using multiplication and addition operators. For asymptotic analysis, we need two expressions, one for the best and one for the worst-case.

Big O Notation

The "O" stands for order and denotes that the growth rates are defined as orders of functions. We could say that a function, T(n), is a big O of F(n) and this is defined like this:

T(n)=O(F(n)) if there are constants, n0, and C in a way that:

T(n) C(F(n)) for all n   n0

The function of the input size n is g(n) and this is based on all large enough values of n, g(n) being upper bound by a constant multiple of f(n). What we want to do is find the smallest growth rate equal to less than f(n). We are only interested in the higher n values; the variable, n, represents the threshold – below that, we're not interested in the growth rate. T(n) is the function that represents F(n), the tight upper bound.

The notation that reads f(n) = O(g(n)) is telling us that O(g(n)) is a set of functions, within which are all the functions with smaller or equal growth rates than f(n). Below, are the common growth rates from low to high. These are sometimes called a function time complexity:

Complexity	Class Name	Operation Examples
O(1)	Constant	get item, set item, append
O(log n)	Logarithmic	find an element in an array that is sorted
O(n)	Linear	insert, copy, iteration, delete
nLogn	Linear-logarithmic	merge-sort, sorting lists
n2	Quadratic	nested loops, finding the shortest path between nodes
n3	Cubic	Matrix multiplication
2n	Exponential	backtracking

Complexity Classes

Normally, we would be looking for the total running time of several basic operations, but it seems that we can take simple operations and combine their complexity classes to determine the class of combined operations that are somewhat more complex. The goal is to look at the combined statements in a method or a function to find the time complexity of executing multiple operations. The easiest way of combining complexity classes is to add them and this happens when the operations are sequential.

Let's say that we have a pair of operations that insert an element in a list and then proceed to sort the list. When the item is inserted, it happens in $O(n)$ time while sorting happens in $O(n\log n)$ time. The time complexity can be written as $O(n + n\log n)$. However, because we are focusing only on the high order term, we can work with just $O(n\log n)$.

Let's then assume that we use a while loop to repeat an operation; we would take the complexity class and multiply it by how many times the operation is done. For example, an operation that has a time complexity of $O(f(n))$ is repeated $O(n)$ times; both complexities are multiplied as follows:

This loop then has a time complexity of O(n2) * O(n) = O(n * n2) = O(n3). All we have done is multiply the operation's time complexity by the number of times that operation was executed. A loop's running time is no more than the combined running time of all the statements in the loop multiplied by the iterations. Assuming both loops will run n times, a single nested loop runs in n2 time.

For example:

```
for i in range(0,n):
    for j in range(0,n)
        #statements
```

Each of these statements is a constant (c) that is executed nn times. The running time can thus be expressed as;cn n + cn2 = O(n2)

For all consecutive statements in a nested loop, the time complexity for each of the statements is added and then multiplied by the iterations of the statement. For example:

Amortized Analysis

Sometimes we are not bothered so much about the time complexity of an individual operation; sometimes we want to know what the average running time is of a sequence of operations. This is called amortized analysis and, as you will see later, it is not the same as the average case analysis because it doesn't assume anything about the data distribution of any input values. What it does do is take the change in the state of the data structures into account. For example, sorting a list should make finding operations faster in the future. The amortized analysis considers the change in the state because the sequence of operations is analyzed; it doesn't just aggregate single operations.

What amortized analysis does is determines the upper bound on runtime and it does this by imposing each operation in a sequence with an artificial cost. Each of these costs is then combined. This takes consideration of the fact that the initial expense of an operation can then make future operations much cheaper.

When there are multiple small operations that are expensive, like sorting, and multiple options that are cheaper, like lookups, using worst-case analysis can give us pessimistic results. This is because worst-case assumes that each of the lookups should compare every element until a match is found.

Up to now, we have assumed that we have random input data and we only looked at how the input size affects the runtime. There are two more common algorithm analyses we can look at:

- Average Case Analysis
- Benchmarking

Average case analysis takes some assumptions about the relative frequency of the different input values and determines the average running time. Benchmarking is when a previously agreed set of inputs is used to measure performance.

Both approaches rely on some domain knowledge. For a start, we would need to know what the expected or the typical datasets are. Ultimately, we will be trying to improve the performance by finetuning to an application setting that is highly specific.

A straightforward benchmarking approach would be to time how long the algorithm takes to finish given different input sizes. This is entirely dependent on what hardware the algorithm is run on; the faster the processor, the better the result. However, the relative growth rates that come with the increases in the input rates will retain the characteristics of the algorithm and not the platform they run on.

5. How To Use Your Python Skills

There are many ways that you can use the skills that you have just learned to be able to try Python and use it for yourself. Once you know how to use Python, you can do all of your own programming, and that will give you the help that you need to be able to get started with your career in programming. Gone are the days where you need to rely on programs that are created by other people or the "expert" help of people who really can't do much to help you. After reading this book, you will be more than just a beginner, and you will be able to use that to your benefit so that you can do everything from providing yourself with a service to making a lucrative income.

Power a Social Media Site

With the capabilities that Python has, you can not only build an entire social media site but also power it.

While many of the other social media sites have moved onto "bigger" languages that are just a few steps up from Python, Instagram still uses Python to power everything that they do. You will be able to do the same, and hopefully, one day have a social media site that is just as famous as Instagram.

Create a Fun Game for Friends

Throughout this book, you learned the way to make different things and give people choices for what they were going to put into your input areas. These are all choices that they can make, but you can benefit by putting them into a game. Whether you want to be a game creator or not is irrelevant. Building a game for your friends to play online (or off!) is a great way to practice your Python skills and have a better chance at building really cool stuff in the future.

In the beginning, you can start with a very basic game. Users are asked input questions, and the output is all based on that information. The better you get at writing Python, the more advanced your games can be. You may even be able to make something that is comparable to your favorite video game. From there, take your skills to a different place and you'll be a true Python master in no time!

Learn Insider Secrets

There are no real secrets of Python, but as you begin to work with more codes and try new things out, you will be able to learn some of the quirks that the language comes with so that you can try new things and you'll be able to find out some of the things that the most advanced Python users have. This is a great way to learn new things, try out new codes, and give yourself a chance at doing more with the Python language so that you can take it to the next level.

You can also use Python if you want to enter any program through the back door. While it isn't necessarily the best hacking language that is available for you to try, it is something that you can get very comfortable with getting the specifics on other programs with. It will give you a chance to do much more than simply creating websites, programs, or other things that can sometimes be complicated for you to figure out.

The Language of Google

The language that Google uses is the same language that you are beginning to learn all about. Google is one of the biggest sites on the Internet and possibly the most-visited around the world depending on which statistics you look at. If something as big as Google continues to use Python, then it is a relatively good language to learn.

One thing that you can do is teach yourself how the programming and the codes of Google work. While I wouldn't necessarily suggest trying to compete with Google, you can try to learn more so that you will be able to give yourself a better chance with the options that you have. One of those options would be to try and get a job with Google. Having Python knowledge will help you get a job at nearly any tech-related industry.

Build on Your Knowledge

For many people who just want to know the basics, Python is the end of the line. For others, though, it can be a simple stepping stone to learning more coding language. The majority of people who know the more complicated methods of writing in different code languages started with Python and continue to use it while they are working on different languages.

One of the best parts of being able to use Python to build on the knowledge that you have is that you will always be able to learn more from what you are doing and what you have done with Python. None of the languages that are present in today's world are exactly the same, but knowing one code language will often help you to have a better chance at learning a different one.

Make Money

You don't need another company to be able to show you what to do. This is something that you can do once you master Python and something that is going to be very lucrative depending on how you market yourself.

How to Make Money with Python

Once you have learned Python and the way to make sure that you are creating the perfect program, you will be able to start making money with it. Some people may be tempted to go to companies or businesses and ask them to hire them, but that is not where the real money is.

If you want to truly make money with Python, you need to go your own way and make sure that you are doing it right.

Follow these steps to launch your Python career and earn yourself some financial freedom:

Practice

You will absolutely need to practice with Python. You should not try to go out on your own and start a career after reading this book. Read it again. Try new things on Python. Use variations. Look for new codes. All of these will help you to practice and will give you a chance to see which aspects of Python you are good at and which ones could stand to have a little more practice.

Remember, though, that you will get better if you practice a lot.

Create

It is necessary to create things with Python for yourself before you are able to create them for other people. Since you have a skill, you will need to use it for your own good first. Try to make some games, design a program, and prepare yourself to do more for other people. Think of things that people may want you to create for them and do them for yourself. This will allow you to keep practicing but will also put your knowledge to work so that you can use it later on when you are listing the work that you did.

List

Create a list of all of the things that you have done with Python. Build a site using Python and make sure that you connect it with the things that you have done. Give yourself a killer domain name and then design the site so that it is seamless. This is your portfolio. It is where you will direct people to when you are talking about your services. It is also where your work will be showcased, so be sure to always show off your best Python programming.

Advertise

Advertising yourself is as simple as advertising a business. Let them know that they need you, not the other way around. If you offer a service that they need and that they can't refuse, you'll be able to advertise yourself much more easily. It is a good idea to try and make sure that you are doing what you can to advertise yourself in a positive light. Use social media, networking opportunities, and even chances offline to advertise the fact that you are able to do programming. Always remember to include the link to your portfolio so that they can see the work that you have done.

Prove Value

Some people may balk at the prices that you are charging them especially if they have never tried to hire a programmer before. Make sure that you show them why it costs so much to hire you. They will be much easier to retain if you can prove that you are valuable.

Negotiate

The chances are that you are going to have to negotiate especially when you are first getting started with your Python programming career. There is nothing wrong with this even if you think that you are worth more than what someone wants to pay you for the work that you are doing. Keep all of this in mind when you start to forget why you were doing it in the first place. The negotiation process can be tricky, but you'll be able to do the most if you do negotiate in the beginning.

Collect

Sit back and collect on the money that you can make from programming. You stand to have a very lucrative career if you make sure that you always do the best work possible, you provide people with a reason to want to hire you, and you show them that you are extremely valuable when it comes to the services that you offer. Are you ready for financial freedom thanks to Python?

6. Development Tools

As with every work environment, to increase our productivity in Scientific Computing there are several tools beyond the programming language. In this chapter we will talk about the most important tools of Python.

IPython

The interactive use of Python is extremely valuable. Other environments geared toward scientific computing, such as Matlab™, R, Mathematica™, among others, use interactive mode as their primary mode of operation. Those who want to do the same with Python can greatly benefit from IPython.

IPython is a very sophisticated version of the Python shell designed to make interactive use of the Python language more aware..

First steps

To start IPython, type the following command:

1 $ ipython [options] archives

Many of the options that control IPython's operation are not passed on the command line; they are specified in the IPythonrc file within the /.IPython directory.

Four IPython options are considered unique and should appear first, before any other options: -gthread, -qthread, -wthread, -pylab. The first three options are for the interactive use of modules in the construction of GUIs (graphical interfaces), respectively GTK, Qt, WxPython.

These options start IPython on a separate thread to allow interactive control of graphics. This option will execute from pylab import on startup, and allows graphs to be displayed without having to invoke the show () command, but will execute scripts that contain show () at the correct time.

After one of the four options above has been specified, the regular options may follow in any order. All options may be abbreviated to the shortest unambiguous form, but must be case sensitive (as in Python and Bash languages, by the way). One or two hyphens may be used in specifying options.

All options can be set to be turned off (if enabled by default).

Due to a large number of existing options, we will not list them here. consult the IPython documentation to learn about them. However, some options may appear throughout this section and will be explained as they arise.

Magic Commands

One of the most useful features of IPython is the concept of magic commands. In the IPython console, any line beginning with the% character is considered a call to a magic command. For example, %autoindent turns on automatic indentation within IPython.

There is an option that is enabled by default in IPythonrc, called automagic. With this function, magic commands can be called without %, i.e. autoindent is understood as % autoindent. User-defined variables can mask magic commands.

Therefore, if I set a variable autoindent = 1, the word autoindent is no longer recognized as a magic command but as the name of the variable I created. However, I can still call the magic command by placing the% character at the beginning.

The user can extend the magic command set with their own creations. See the IPython documentation on how to do this.

The magic command% magic returns an explanation of the existing magic commands.

%Exit Exits the IPython console.

%Pprint Turns text formatting on / off.

%Quit Exit IPython without asking for confirmation.

%alias Give me a synonym for a command.

You can use %1 to represent the line on which the alias command was called, for example:

1 In [2]: alias all echo " Input between parenthesis: (% l) "

2   In [3]:   all Hello World

3 Input between parenthesis: (Hello world)

%autocall Turns on / off mode that lets you call functions without parentheses. For example: fun 1 becomes fun (1).

%autoindent Turns on / off auto-indentation.

%automagic Auto magic on / off.

%bg Executes a background command on a separate thread. For example:%bg func (x, y, z = 1). As soon as execution starts, a message is printed on the console informing you of the job number. Thus, you can access job result # 5 through the jobs.results [5] command.

IPython has a task manager accessible through the job object. For more information on this object, type jobs ?. IPython lets you automatically complete a partially typed command. To see all methods of the job object try typing jobs.following the <TAB> key.

%bookmark Manages the IPython bookmark system. To learn more about bookmarks type% bookmark ?.

%cd Changes directory.

%colors Change the color scheme.

%cpaste Pastes and executes a preformatted clipboard block. The block must be terminated by a line containing −−.

%dhist Print directory history.

%ed Synonym for% edit

%edit Opens an editor and executes the edited code on exit. This command accepts several options, see the documentation.

The editor to be opened by the% edit command is whatever is set in the $ EDITOR environment variable. If this variable is not clear, IPython will open vi. If you do not specify a file name, IPython will open a Temporary file for editing. The% edit command has some conveniences.

For example, if we define a fun function in an edit session when exiting and executing code, this function will remain clear in the current namespace. Then we can just type %edit fun and IPython will open the file containing it, automatically placing the cursor on the relevant line. When you leave this editing session, the edited function will be updated.

1 In [6]: %ed

2 IPython will make a temporary file named:/tmp/ipython_edit_GuUWr_.py

3done. Executing edited code.. .

4   Out [6]: "def fun():\ n   p r in t ` fun'\ n   \ ndef fun():\ nprint 'fun'\ n"

5

6 In [7]: fun()

7 fun

8

9 In [8]: fun()

10 fun

11

12 In [9]: % ed fun

13done. Executing edited code.. .

%hist Synonym for% historic.

%history Prints the command history. Previous commands can also be accessed via the _i <n> variable, which is the only historical command.

1 In [1]: %hist

2 1: _ip.magic ("%hist")

3

4 In [2]: %hist

5   1: _ip.magic ("%hist")

6   2: _ip.magic ("%hist")

IPython has a sophisticated session registration system. This system is controlled by the following magic commands:

%logon, %logoff, %logstart and %logstate. For more information see the documentation.

%lsmagic Lists the available magic commands.

%macro Give a set of command lines as a macro for later use: % macro test 1 2 or %macro macro2 44-47 49.

%p Synonym for print.

%pdb turns on / off interactive debugger.

%pdef Prints the header of any callable object. If the object is a class, it returns information about the class's constructor.

%pdoc Prints the docstring of an object.

%pfile Prints the file where the object is set.

%psearch searches for objects in namespaces.

%psource prints the source code of an object. The object must have been imported from a file.

%quickref shows a quick reference guide

%quit exits IPython.

%r repeats the previous command.

%rehash updates the synonym table with all entries in

$ PATH. This command does not check to execute
permissions and whether the entries are even files.
%rehashx does this, but is slower.

%rehashdir adds the executables from the specified
directories to the synonym table.

%rehashx updates the thesaurus with all executable
files in $ PATH.

%reset resets the namespace by removing all user
names.

%run runs the specified file inside IPython as a
program.

%runlog runs files as logs.

%save saves a set of lines to a file.

%sx runs a command on the Linux console and
captures its output.

%store stores variables to be available in a future session.

%time times the execution of a command or expression.

%timeit times the execution of a command or expression using the timeit module.

%unalias removes a synonym.

%upgrade upgrades the IPython installation.

%who prints all interactive variables with a minimum of formatting.

%who_ls returns a list of all interactive variables.

%whos is similar to% who, with more information about each variable.

To top it off, IPython is an excellent interactive working environment for scientific computing, especially when invoked with the -pylab option. The numpy main package is also exposed in pylab mode. Numpy sub-packages need to be imported manually.

Code Editors

When editing Python programs, a good code editor can make a big difference in productivity. Due to the significance of the blanks for the language, an editor that maintains consistent code indentation is very important to avoid bugs.

It is also desirable for the editor to know Python's rules of indentation, for example: indent after:, indent with spaces rather than tabs. Another desirable feature is the colorization of the code to emphasize the language syntax. This feature dramatically increases the readability of the code.

Editors that can be successfully used for editing Python programs fall into two basic categories: generic editors and Python-specialized editors. In this section, we'll look at the key features of some editors in each category.

Generic Editors

There are a number of text editors available for the Gnu / Linux environment. The vast majority of them meet our basic requirements for automatic indentation and colorization. I selected some that stand out in my preference for usability and versatility.

Emacs: Incredibly complete and versatile editor, it works as an integrated development environment. Must have python-mode installed. For those with no prior experience with Emacs, I recommend that the Easymacs1 package be installed as well. This package makes the Emacs interface much easier, especially for adding standard CUA keyboard shortcuts. You can also use IPython within Emacs.

Scite: Lightweight and aware editor, supports Python well (runs the script with <F5>) as well as several other languages. It allows you to configure C and Fortran compilation commands, which makes it easier to develop extensions. Completely configurable (Figure 4.1).

Ideal for use in conjunction with IPython (% edit command).

Jedit: I have included Jedit in this list as it supports Jython development (see Section 5.5). Aside from that, it is a very powerful editor for java and not as heavy as Eclipse.

Kate / Gedit Standard editors of KDE and Gnome respectively. Good for casual use, Kate has the advantage of a built-in console.

Specialized Publishers

Python publishers tend to be more of the IDE (integrated development environment) type, offering features that only make sense for managing midsize to large projects, but too much for editing a simple script.

Boa-Constructor: Boa-constructor is an IDE, aimed at projects wishing to use WxPython as a graphical interface. In this respect it is perfect, allowing visual construction of the interface,

Gnu Nano Editor

generating all the code associated with the interface. It also features an excellent debugger for Python programs and supports extension modules written in other languages, such as Pyrex or C .

Eric: Eric is also a Python IDE with the PyQt interface. It has functional integration with the Qt Designer interface generator, making it easy to develop graphical interfaces with this tool. It also has a great debugger. In addition Eric offers many other functions, such as integration with version control, version control systems, storage generators, etc.

Pydev (Eclipse): Pydev is an IDE for Python and Jython developed as an Eclipse plugin. For those who already have experience with the Eclipse platform, it may be a good alternative, otherwise it may be much more complicated to operate than the alternatives mentioned above. In terms of functionality, it matches Eric and Boa-constructor.

IDE Boa-Constructor

Software Version Control

When developing software on any scale, we experience a process of progressive improvement in which software goes through various versions. In this process, it is very common, at a certain stage, to recover some functionality that was present in an earlier version, and which for some reason has been deleted from the code.

Another challenge in the development of scientific products (software or others) is teamwork around the same object (often a program). Usually each team member works individually and presents their results to the team in regular meetings. What to do when modifications developed by different members of the same team become incompatible? Or even when two or more employees are working on different parts of a program but need each other to work?

The type of tool we will introduce in this section seeks to solve or minimize the above problems and can also be applied to the collaborative development of other types of documents, not just programs. Since this is a Python-based book, let's use a version control system developed entirely in Python Mercurial 2.

In practice the mechanism behind all version control systems is very similar. Migrating from one to another is a matter of learning new names for the same operations. In addition, the daily use of the version control system involves only two or three commands.

IDE Eric

Understanding Mercurial

Mercurial is a decentralized version control system, meaning there is no notion of a central server where code is deposited.

Diagram of a Mercurial Repository

Code repositories are directories that can be cloned from one machine to another.

So what does a repository consist of? To simplify our explanation, consider that the repository has already been created or cloned from someone who created it. We'll see how to create a repository from scratch later.

The archive contains the complete project history. The working directory contains a copy of the project files at a certain point in time (for example, in revision 2). It is in the working directory that the researcher works and updates the files.

After a commit, as the working directory sources did not correspond to the latest project revision, Mercurial automatically creates a script in the file. With that we have two lines of development going in parallel, with our working directory belonging to the branch started by revision 4.

Mercurial groups changes sent by a user (via commit) into an atomic changeset, which constitutes a review.

Ana's Repository

But since Mercurial allows the same project to be developed in parallel, the revision numbers for different developers could differ. Therefore each revision also receives a global identifier consisting of a forty digit hexadecimal number.

In addition to ramifications, merge between branches can occur at any time. Whenever there is more than one branch under development, Mercurial will name the most recent revisions of each branch (heads). Among these, the one with the largest revision number will be considered the tip of the repository.

Example of use:

In these examples, we will explore the most common operations in a collaborative development environment using Mercurial. Let's start with our first developer, called Ana.

Our second developer, Brad, has just joined the team and clones the repository Ana5.

1 $ hg clonessh:// machine of ana/project my project

2 requesting all changes

Note: We assume here that Ana's machine is running a ssh server

    Modifications by Brad
    Modifications of Ana
3 adding change sets

4 adding manifests

5 adding File changes

6 added 4 change sets with 4 changes to 2 Files

Valid URLs:

file://

http://

https://

ssh://

static-http://

After the above command, Brad will receive a complete copy of Ana's file, but his working directory, my project, will remain independent.

Brad then decides to pull Ana's repository to synchronize it with his own.

1 $ hg pull

Updated Brad Repository

2   pulling from ssh://machineofana/project

3 searching for changes

4 adding change sets

5 adding manifests

6 adding File changes

7 added 1 change sets with 1 changes to 1 Files

8 (run 'hg heads 'to see heads, 'hg merge 'to merge)

The hg pull command, if not specifying the source, will pull from the source from which the local repository was cloned. This command will update the local file, but not the working directory.

As Ana's changes were the last ones added to Brad's repository, this revision becomes the tip of the Archive.

Brad now wants to merge his development branch with the tip of his Archive that corresponds to the modifications made by Ana. Usually, after pulling modifications, we run a hg update to synchronize our working directory with the newly updated Archive. So Brad does that.

1 $ hg update

2 this update spans a branch affecting the following Files:

3hello.py (resolve)

Brad's Repository after the Merger

4   aborting update spanning branches!

5 (use 'hg merge' to merge across branches or 'hg update −C' to lose changes)

Due to the ramification in the Brad Archive, the update command does not know which branch to merge the existing modifications into Brad's working directory. To solve this, Brad will need to merge the two branches. Fortunately this is a trivial task.

1 $ hg merge tip

2 merging hello.py

In the merge command, if no revision is specified, the working directory is a branch head and, because there is only one other head, the two heads will be merged. Otherwise a revision must be specified.

Ready!

Creating A Repository

To create a repository from scratch, you only need one command:

1 $ hg init

When the directory is created, a directory named .hg is created within the working directory. Mercurial will store all repository information in the .hg directory. The contents of this directory should not be changed by the user.

Additional Information

Of course, many other things can be done with a version control system. The reader is encouraged to consult the Mercurial documentation to find out. For quick reference, use the hg help -v <command> command with any command from the list below.

add add the specified archive (s) in the next commit.

addremove Add all new files, removing the missed before.

annotate Shows information about file line modifications.

archive Creates an unversioned (compressed) file from a specified revision.

backout **Reverses the effects of a previous modification. branch Changes or shows the name of the current branch.**

branches List all branches of the repository.

bundle **Creates a compressed file containing all modifications not present in another repository.**

cat Returns the specified file as it was in a given revision.

clone Replicates a repository.

commit Files all modifications or specified files.

copy Copies the specified files to another directory on the next commit.

diff Shows differences between revisions or between specified files.

Export Print header and differences for one or more modification sets.

grep Search for words in specific files and revisions.

heads Show current heads.

help Show help for a command, extension, or command list.

identify Print information about the current working copy.

***import* Imports an ordered set of updates (patches). [This command is the counterpart of Export.]**

incoming Shows new sets of modifications existing in a given repository.

init **Creates a new repository in the specified directory. If the directory does not exist, it will be created.**

locate Finds files.

log Shows revision history for the repository as a whole or for some files

manifest Returns the manifest (controlled file list) of the current or other revision.

merge Merges the working directory with another revision.

outgoing Shows set of modifications not present in the destination repository.

parents Show the parents of the working or revision directory.

paths Show symbolic path names.

pull Pulls updates from the specified source.

push **Sends modifications to the specified destination repository. [It is the counterpart of pull.]**

recover Undoes a broken transaction.

remove Removes the files specified at the next commit. rename Renames files; Equivalent to copy + remove.

revert Revert files to the state they were in a given revision.

rollback Undoes the last transaction in this repository.

root Prints the root of the current working directory. serve Exports the directory via HTTP.

showconfig Shows the combined configuration of all hgrc files.

status Shows modified files in the working directory.

tag Adds a marker for the current or other revision.

tags Lists repository bookmarks.

tip Shows the tip revision.

unbundle Applies a modification file.

update Updates or merges the working directory.

*Verify*Verifies the integrity of the repository.

version Returns version and copyright information.

7. The Best Python Libraries To Use With Data Science

Now that we know a bit about the basics that come with the Python language, it is important that we spend some time learning the best libraries and extensions that we are able to add into the mix to make sure that Python is going to work the way that we would like for data science. The regular library that comes with Python can do a lot of amazing things, but it is not going to be able to handle all of the graphing, mathematics, and the machine learning that we need with data science.

The good news here though is that there are a few other libraries that we are able to work with that utilize Python and can help with machine learning and data science together. All of these are going to help us handle tasks in a slightly different manner so take a look at them and how they are meant to work with Python and data science. The best libraries that can help you to get this work done will include:

NumPy and SciPy

If you want to do any kind of work with machine learning or data science with Python, you have to make sure that you work with the NumPy and the SciPy library. Both of these are going to be the basis of many of the other libraries that we are going to talk about here, which is why it is likely that when you work with data science, you are going to also add in a bit of library as well.

First, we will look at NumPy, which is going to stand for Numeric and Scientific Computation. This is a useful library because it is going to lay down some of the basic premises that we need for doing any kind of scientific computing with data science in Python. This library can also help us to get ahold of some functions that have been precompiled for us, and it is fast for handling any numerical and mathematical routine process that you would like to do.

Then there is also the Scientific Python library, which we call SciPy, that goes along with NumPy in many cases. This is the kind of library that you want to work with to add in some kind of competitive edge to what you are doing in machine learning. This happens when you work to enhance some of the useful functions for things like regression and minimization to name a few.

Matplotlib

As you are going through data science and Python, there are going to be times when you will want to work with a graph or a chart or some other kind of visual. This is going to make it easier to see the information that is found in the text, in a glance and the matplotlib will be able to make some of these graphs for you in no time.

The matplotlib extension is going to provide us with all of the parts that we need to take the info and turn it into the visualizations that you need for your data. This library is going to work with pretty much any of the different types of visualizations that you need from a histogram, bar charts, error charts, line graphs, and more.

The Scikit-Learn library

The Scikit-Learn is the library that we are going to take a look at next. This is a great one to go with when it comes to machine learning. This is because the package that comes with this library is going to provide us with a lot of machine learning algorithms and more that we can use to really get data science to work. It is going to include a lot of different parts that can ensure we analyze the information that is fed into the algorithm in a proper manner.

One other benefit that we are going to see when it comes to this kind of library is that it is easy to distribute, which means it works well in commercial and academic kind of settings, and there are not a lot of dependencies that go with it. The interface is concise and consistent, which make it easier to work with, and you will find that the most common of the machine learning algorithms are already inside, making it easier to create some of the models you need for data science.

Pandas

The next library in Python that you want to work with to make machine learning and data science do what you would like. Pandas are going to stand for the Python Data Analysis Library, which helps us to do a lot of the work that is needed in the Python world. This is an open-sourced tool that helps us with some of the data structures that are needed to do data analysis. You can use this library to add in the right tools and data structures to make sure your data analysis is complete, and many industries like to work with this one to help out with some different processes like finance, statistics, engineering, and social science.

This Pandas library is going to be really adaptable, which makes it really great for getting a ton of work done in less time. It can also help you work with any kind of data that you are able to bring in, no matter what kind of source you are getting that info from, making it a lot easier to work with. This library is going to come with many different features that you can enjoy and some of the best ones are going to include:

1. You can use the Pandas library to help reshape the structures of your data.
2. You can use the Pandas library to label series, as well as tabular data, to help us see an automatic alignment.
3. You can use the Pandas library to help with heterogeneous indexing of the info and it is also useful when it comes to systematic labeling of the data as well.

4. You can use this library because it can hold onto the capabilities of identifying and then fixing any of the data that is missing.
5. This library provides us with the ability to load and then save data from more than one format.
6. You can easily take some of the data structures that come out of Python and NumPy and convert them into the objects that you need to Pandas objects.

TensorFlow

TensorFlow, one of the best Python libraries for data science, is a library that was released by Google Brain. It was written out mostly in the language of C++, but it is going to include some bindings in Python, so the performance is not something that you are going to need to worry about. One of the best features that comes with this library is going to be some of the flexible architecture that is found in the mix, which is going to allow the programmer to deploy it with one or more GPUs or CPUs in a desktop, mobile, or server device, while using the same API the whole time.

Not many, if any, of the other libraries that we are using in this chapter, will be able to make this kind of claim. This library is also unique in that it was developed by the Google Brain project, and it is not used by many other programmers. However, you do need to spend a bit more time to learn the API compared to some of the other libraries. In just a few minutes, you will find that it is possible to work with this TensorFlow library in order to implement the design of your network, without having to fight through the API as you do with other options.

The Keras library

If you are looking for a Python library that can handle data science and data analytics that is also easy for the user to work with, then this is the library for you. It is able to handle a lot of the different processes that come with the other libraries, but it keeps in mind the user, rather than the machine when it comes to designing the interface and the other parts that you use within this coding library. The user experience is easy, the interface is designed to only need a few clicks to get the processes done and it all comes together to make data science and machine learning as easy as possible.

This library is going to work a lot of the modules that are needed for machine learning. You can work with a module that is on its own, or you can combine together a few modules in order to get the results that you would like. There is a lot of flexibility that comes with using this kind of library, and that is one of the many reasons that so many programmers like to use it when completing work with Python data science.

These are just a few of the different libraries that you are able to use along with the Python coding language to get some of your data science and machine learning work done. These libraries all work on slightly different types of processes when it comes to data science, which is going to make them so much easier to work with overall. Take a look at each one, and see just how they can all come together to provide you with the results that you want in your data analytics project.

8. Lists And Dictionaries

We have learned quite a lot ever since we started with this book. We have gone through operators, we learned about various data types, and we also looked at loops and statements. During all of this, we did mention the word 'list' and represented these with a square bracket instead of curly or round brackets. This chapter will now explore and explain what exactly lists are. We will also come across the term "dictionaries" and hopefully, by the end of this chapter, we should be familiarized with the core concepts of these and how they are vital to programming of any kind.

Remember, this book is aimed only for absolute Python beginners. For more advanced references, you are encouraged to seek appropriate knowledge in books or on online learning platforms specific to your requirements.

A Look into What Lists Are

Let us go ahead and create an imaginary family that comprises of Smith, Mary, their daughter Alicia, and their son Elijah. How would we do that? Begin by creating a variable named family as shown below:

----

family = ['Smith', 'Mary', 'Alicia', 'Elijah']

Using the [] brackets, we provided the data to this variable. Now, this specific variable holds more than one name within it. This is where lists come to the rescue. Through listing, we can store as many values within a variable as we like. In this case, we can stick to four only.

If you now use the print command to print 'family', you should see the following:

======

['Smith', 'Mary', 'Alicia', 'Elijah']

======

The values or names stored within the brackets are called as items. To call on the item or to check what item is stored on a specific index number, you can use the method we had used earlier in strings.

----

print(family[0])

======

Smith

======

Instead of showing 'S', the complete name was shown. Similarly, if you use the other functions such as the len() function, it would provide you with the length of the list. In this case, it would should you that there are four items in this list. Let us try that out for ourselves.

----

print(len(family))

=====

4

=====

You can use the [x:y] where x and y are ranges you can set. This can be helpful if the list you are working on contains hundreds of entries. You can only filter out the ones you would like to view. You can jump straight to the end of the list by using [-1] to see the last entry. The combinations are endless.

Here is a little brain-teaser. Suppose we have numerous numbers in a list, around 100. They are not listed chronologically and we do not have time to scroll through each one of them. We need to find out which of these numbers is the highest. How can we do that?

This is where lists, loops, and if statements come together. How? Let us look into it right away:

----

numbers = [312, 1434, 68764, 4627, 84, 470, 9047, 98463, 389, 2]

high = numbers[0]

for number in numbers:

    if number > high:

        high = number

print(f"The highest number is {high}")

======

The highest number is 98463

======

Time to put our thinking cap on and see what just happened.

We started out by providing some random numbers. One of these was surely the highest. We created a variable and assigned it the first item of the list of numbers as its value. We do not know whether this item holds the highest value.

Moving ahead, we initiated a 'for' loop where we created a loop variable called number. This number would iterate each value from numbers. We used an 'if' statement to tell the interpreter that if the loop variable 'number' is greater than our currently set highest number 'high', it should immediately replace that with the value it holds.

Once the program was run, Python sees we assigned 'high' a value of the first item which is 312. Once the loop and if statement begin, Python analyzes if the first item is greater than the value of the variable 'high'. Surely, 312 is not greater than 312 itself. The loop does not alter the value and ends. Now, the 'for' loop restarts, this time with the second item value. Now, the value has changed. This time around, when the 'if'

156

statement is executed, Python sees that our variable has a lower value than the one it is currently working on. 312 is far less than 1434. Therefore, it executes the code within the statement and replaces the value of our variable to the newly found higher value. This process will continue on until all values are cross-checked and finally the largest value is maintained. Then, only the largest value will be printed for us.

2-D Lists

In Python, we have another kind of list that is called the two-dimensional list. If you are someone who is willing to master data sciences or machine learning, you will need to use these quite a lot. The 2-D list is quite a powerful tool. Generally, when it comes to maths, we have what are called matrixes. These are arrays of numbers formed in rectangular form within large brackets.

Unlike your regular lists, these contain rows and columns of values and data as shown here:

----

matrix = [

```
    [19, 11, 91],

    [41, 25, 54],

    [86, 28, 21]

]
```

In an easier way, imagine this as a list which contains a number of lists inside. As illustrated above, each row is now acting as a separate list. Had this been a regular list, we could have printed a value using the index number. How do you suppose we can have the console print out the value of our first item within the first list?

----

print(matrix[0][0])

Using the above, you can now command interpreter to only print out the first value stored within the first list. The first zero within the first [] tells the interpreter the number of list to access. Following that is the second bracket set which further directs the search to the index number of the item. In this case, we were aiming to print out 19 and thus, 19 will be our result.

Take a moment and try to print out 25, 21, and 86 separately. If you were able to do this, good job.

You can change the values of the items within the list. If you know the location of the said item, you can use the name of the variable followed by the [x][y] position of the item. Assign a new number by using the single equal to mark and the value you wish for it to have.

The 2-D lists are normally used for slightly advanced programming where you need to juggle quite a lot of values and data types. However, it is best to keep these in mind as you never know when you may actually need to use them.

List Methods

Somewhere in the start, we learned about something called methods. These are extra methods which are available that can be used with the said variable or object. So far, we have seen how to use the .lower or the .upper methods for strings. Those methods change the input of the user to either lower or upper case. For lists, things are a little different.

To start off, let us go back to the PyCharm and create our own list of random numbers. Let's use the following number sequence:

```
----------

numbers = [11, 22, 33, 44, 55, 66, 77]

----------
```

We are not going to print this out to our console. Instead, we would like to see what possible methods are available for us to use. In the next line, type the name of the variable followed by the dot operator "." to access the methods.

Quite a lot, aren't they? We won't be needing all of them right now. We will just focus on the ones which are more commonly used and that every beginner should know. Let us type the append method.

The append method allows us to add an entry or a value to the list under the selected variable. Go ahead and add any number of your choice. Done? Now try and print the variable named 'numbers' and see what happens.

You should be able to see a number added at the end of the list. Good, but what if you don't wish to add a number at the end? What if you want it to be somewhere close to the start?

To do that, we need a method called insert.

----

numbers.insert()

In order for us to execute this properly, we will need to first provide this method with the index position where we wish for the new number to be added. If you wish to add it to the start, use zero or if you wish to add it to any other index, use that number. Follow this number by a comma and the number itself.

Now, if you print the numbers variable, you should be able to see the new number added exactly where you wanted.

----

numbers.insert(2, 20)

print(numbers)

=====

[11, 22, 20, 33, 44, 55, 66, 77]

=====

Similarly, you can use a method called remove to delete any number you wish to be removed from the list.

When using the remove method, do note that it will only remove the number where it first occurred. It will not remove the same number which might have repeated later on within the same list as shown here:

----

numbers = [11, 22, 33, 44, 55, 66, 77, 37, 77]

numbers.remove(77)

print(numbers)

=====

[11, 22, 33, 44, 55, 66, 37, 77]

=====

For any given reason, if you decide you no longer require the list content, you can use the clear command. This command does not require you to pass any object within the parentheses.

----

numbers.clear()

Using another method, you can check on the index number of a specific value's first occurrence.

----

numbers.index(44)

If you run the above, you will get '3' as a result. Why? The index position of three contains the number 44 in the list we used earlier. If you put in a value that is not within the defined list values, you will end up with an error as shown here:

=====

 print(numbers.index(120))

ValueError: 120 is not in list

=====

There is another useful method that helps you quite a lot when you are dealing with a bunch of numbers of other data types. In case you are not too sure and you wish to find out whether a specific number exists within a list, you can use the 'in' operator as shown:

----

numbers = [11, 22, 33, 44, 55, 66, 77, 37, 77]

print(43 in numbers)

What do you think the result will be? An error? You might be wrong. This is where the result will show 'False'. This is a boolean value and is indicating that the number we wanted to search for does not exist in our list. If the number did exist, the return boolean value would have been 'True'.

Let us assume that we have a large number of items in the list and we wish to find out just how many times a specific number is being used or repeated within the said list. There is a way we can command Python to do it for us. This is where you will use the 'count' method.

In our own list above, we have two occurrences where the number 77 is used. Let us see how we can use this method to find out both the instances.

----

print(numbers.count(77))

The result will now state '2' as our result. Go ahead and add random numbers to the list with a few repeating ones. Use the count method to find out the number of occurrences and see how the command works for you. The more you practice, the more you will remember.

Now we have seen how to locate, change, add, clear, and count the items in the list. What if we wish to sort the entire list in ascending or descending order? Can we do that?

With the help of the sort method, you can actually have that carried out. The sort() method by default will only sort the data into ascending order. If you try and access the method within a print command, the console will show 'none' as your return. To have this done correctly, always use the sort method before or after the print command. To reverse the order, use the reverse() method. This method, just like the sort() method, does not require you to pass any object within the brackets.

Tuples

In Python, we use lists to store various values and these values can be accessed, changed, modified, or removed at will, whenever we like. That certainly might not be the best thing to know if you intend to use data that is essential in nature. To overcome that, there is a kind of list that will store the data for you but after that, no additional modification will be carried out, even if you try and do it accidentally or intentionally. These are called tuples.

Tuples are a form of list which are very important to know when it comes to Python. Unlike the square bracket representation for lists, these are represented by parentheses ().

----

numbers = (19, 21, 28, 10, 11)

Tuples are known as immutable items. This is because of the fact that you cannot mutate or modify them. Let us deliberately try and modify the value to see what happens.

As soon as you type in the dot operator to access append, remove, and other similar methods, you should see this instead:

```
numbers = (19, 21, 28, 10, 11)
numbers.
    m count(self, x)                              tuple
    m index(self, x, start, end)                 tuple
    m __add__(self, x)                           tuple
    f __annotations__                            object
    p __class__                                  object
    m __contains__(self, x)                      tuple
    m __delattr__(self, name)                    object
    f __dict__                                   object
    m __dir__(self)                              object
    m __eq__(self, o)                            object
    m __format__(self, format_spec)              object
    m __                                         tuple
Press Ctrl+. to choose the selected (or first) suggestion and insert a dot afterwards Next Tip
```

Tuples simply do not have these options anymore. That is because you are trying to modify a value that is secure and locked by Python. You can try another method to see if you can forcefully change the value by doing this:

----

numbers = (19, 21, 28, 10, 11)

numbers[0] = 10

```
print(numbers)
```

======

```
numbers[0] = 10
```

TypeError: 'tuple' object does not support item assignment

======

See how the error came up? The program cannot carry out this change of value, nor can it append the value in any way.

While most of the time you will be working with lists, tuples come in handy to ensure you store values which you know you really don't wish to change accidentally in the future. Think of a shape that you wish to create and maintain throughout the game or website as uniform. You can always call on the values of a tuple and use the values when and where needed.

The only way these values might be changed is if you purposely or unintentionally overwrite them. For example, you had written the values of a tuple within the code and move on hundreds of lines ahead. At this point, you might have forgotten about the earlier values or the fact that you wrote these values previously. You start writing new values by using exactly the same name and start storing new values within them. This is where Python will allow you to overwrite the previously stored values without providing you any errors when you run the program.

The reason that happens is because Python understands that you may wish for a value to change later on and then stay the same for a while until you need to change them yet again. When you execute the program, the initially stored values will continue to remain in use right up until the point where you want them to be changed. In order to do that, you can simply do the following:

----

numbers = (1, 2, 3, 4, 5)

print(numbers)

numbers = (6, 7, 8, 9, 10)

print(numbers)

=======

(1, 2, 3, 4, 5)

(6, 7, 8, 9, 10)

=======

The number values have changed without the program screaming back at us with an error. As long as you know and you do this change on purpose, there is absolutely nothing to worry about. However, should you start typing the same tuple and are about to rewrite it, you will be notified by PyCharm about the existence of the same tuple stored before. Can you guess how? Go ahead and try writing the above example in PyCharm and see how you are notified.

PyCharm will highlight the name of the tuple for you, and that is an indication that you have already used the same number before. If this was the first occurrence, PyCharm will not highlight the name or the values for you at all.

Another Useful Feature: Unpacking

Since we just discussed tuples, it is essential to know about a feature that has further simplified the use of tuples for us. Unpacking is of great help and is quite useful, too. Suppose you have a few values stored in a tuple and you wish to assign each one of them to another variable individually. There are two ways you can do that. Let us look at the first way of doing so and then we will look at the use of unpacking for comparison.

First method:

----

ages = (25, 30, 35, 40)

Drake = ages[0]

Emma = ages[1]

Sully = ages[2]

Sam = ages[3]

If you print these values now, you will see the ages accordingly. This means that the values stored within these individual variables were successfully taken from the tuple as we wanted. However, this was a little longer. What if we can do all of that in just one line?

Second method:

----

ages = (25, 30, 35, 40)

Drake, Emma, Sully, Sam = ages

Now this looks much more interesting. Instead of using a number of lines, we got the same job done within the same line. Each individual variable still received the same age as the first method and each can be called upon to do exactly the same thing. This is how unpacking can work miracles for us. It saves you time and effort and allows for us to maintain a clean, clear, and readable code for reference.

With that said, it is now time for us to be introduced to one of the most important elements within Python that is used both by beginners and experts almost every single time.

Dictionaries

There are times you will come across certain information that is unique and holds a key value. Let us assume that you have to design a software that can store information about customers or clients. This information may include and is not limited to names, numbers, emails, physical addresses, and so on. This is where dictionaries will come into play.

If you had thought that dictionary in Python would be like your everyday dictionary for languages we speak, you might not have been completely wrong here. There is a similarity that we can see in these dictionaries. Every single entry that is made is unique. If an entry tries to replicate itself or if you try to store the same value again, you will be presented with an error.

So how exactly do we use dictionaries? For that, let us switch back to our new best friend, the PyCharm, and start typing a little.

Come up with an imaginary person's name, email address, age, and phone number. Don't start assigning these yet, as we would like to use the dictionary here to do the same. Ready? Okay, let us begin.

```
user_one = {    #Dictionaries are represented by {}

    'name': 'Sam',

    'age': 40,

    'phone': 123456789,
```

'married': False

}

We have entered some information about a virtual character named Sam. You can use the print command and run the dictionary named 'user_one' and the system will print out these values for you.

For dictionaries, we use the colon : sign between values. The object name is placed in a string followed by the colon sign. After that, we use either a string, a number (integer or float), or a boolean value. You can use these to assign every object with its unique key pair. In case you are confused, key pair is just another way of saying the value that is assigned to the object. For example, the key pair for 'name' is 'Sam'.

Now, let us try and see what happens if we add another 'married' value. As soon as you are done typing, the system will highlight it straight away. Note that you can still type in the new value and the system will continue to function. However, the value it will use will be the latest value it can find.

This means that if you initially set the value for married to False and later change it to True, it will only display True.

```
user_one = {    #Dictionaries are represented by {}

    'name': 'Sam',

    'age': 40,

    'phone': 123456789,

    'married': False,

    'married': True

}
print(user_one['married'])
```

=======

True

=======

When it comes to calling values from the dictionary, we use the name of the string instead of the index number. If you try and run the index number zero, you will be presented with a 'KeyError: 0' in the traceback. Can you guess why that happens?

Dictionaries store values which are unique. If you use a number or a name that does not exist within the defined dictionary, you will always end up with an error. You will need to know the exact name or value of the information you are trying to access.

Similarly, if you try to access 'Phone' instead of 'phone', you will get the same error as Python is case-sensitive and will not identify the former as an existing value.

Dictionaries can be updated easily should the situation call for it. Let us assume that we got the wrong phone number for our client stored in 'user_one', we can simply use the following procedure to update the entry right away:

```
user_one['phone'] = 345678910

print(user_one['phone'])
```

You should now be able to see the new number we have stored. There's one little thing you may have noticed right about now when you did this. See the crazy wiggly lines which have appeared? These are here to suggest you rewrite the value instead of updating it separately to keep the code clean. PyCharm will continue to do this every now and then where it feels like you are causing the code to grow complicated. There is no reason for you to panic if you see these lines. However, if the lines are red in color, something is surely wrong and you may need to check on that.

Similarly, if you wish to add new key information to your dictionary, you can do so easily using almost the same process as shown here:

```
----------

user_one['profession'] = 'programmer'

----------
```

It is that easy! Try and print out the information now and you should be able to see this along with all previous entries available to you.

Lastly, you can use a method called 'get' to stop the program from coming back with an error in case you or your program user enters a wrong or a missing value when calling upon a dictionary. You can also assign it a default value like a symbol to notify yourself or the user that this value does not exist or is not identifiable by the program itself. Here is a little example where the user has tried to find out information about 'kids'. We have provided it with a default value of 'invalid':

```
print(user_one.get('kids', 'invalid'))
```

If you run this through, you will be presented with a result that shows an object named 'invalid'. We will make use of this feature in a more meaningful way in our test.

9. How To Handle Unstructured Data With Text Mining

Many times, the data that we are going to work with is going to come to us in an unstructured form. While there can be a lot of valuable information that is hidden in that unstructured data, it is often a big pain to deal with. It is not organized, the formatting is often different based on where you get the information, and it can take a lot of time to get this data ready to go through one of your models or algorithms

This doesn't mean that we want to avoid the unstructured data completely. Our modern world is full of a ton of data, and most of it is going to be unstructured. If you really want to be able to figure out about your data and what is inside of it, and you want to answer some of those big business questions that are important to you, then you have to spend time working with unstructured data.

This means that we need to have some kind of plan in place to help deal with some of the unstructured data that you have. it is not going to be as smooth cut and as easy as what we can see with structured data. But when we are able to combine together a few of the options that we use with data science, specifically what we can do with text mining, we will be able to organize that unstructured data in a manner that is easy to read through, and can give us the results that we would like in the end. So, let's get started.

What is Text Mining

The first thing that we need to take a look at in this kind of process is the idea of text mining. This is often going to be referred to as text data mining and it is going to be the process of extracting and analyzing data when it comes to us in the form of large amounts of text data that is unstructured. The analyzing of text data is part of this process, or we can call it text analytics. Text mining is going to help us to perform a process that is able to identify keywords, topics, patterns, and concepts, as well as some other important attributes, to the data that we are working with.

Then it will extract and analyze the important parts of the data from all of the unstructured text data that we do not need. This analysis can help us to really find some of the valuable insights, the ones that would be hard to identify without some help from text mining.

When we look at the large amounts of data that most companies are collecting on a daily basis, taking the time to manually identify the information that you need from that huge amount of data is impossible. So, being able to use text mining is a great lifesaver for these businesses. This process can actually go through and find the important information that you need, and then you can use this with your algorithms and other options to get the results that you would like.

As the years have gone on, the process of text mining has definitely become more practical and most companies that are working with a data science project are going to use it.

This is mainly because of the big data that we are using today. Those who are using this big data, including data scientists, businesses, and more, will find that they can use this text mining, and deep learning, to make it easier to analyze a very large set of data that is not structured in order to get the important predictions and insights out of it that pertain to them.

Text mining is able to extract and analyze all of the facts, relationships, and assertions that are found in the source of data, as long as they relate to the information that you are working with. This process is going to take that data and turn it into a structured form of data. Now, there are going to be a few different methods that the data scientist is able to use to make this happen including visualization with the help of mind maps, charts, and HTML tables, integration with the structured data that you are already storing in a database, and other machine learning systems that are set up to do more of the classification that you are looking for.

As we work through this, you may find that the sources of analyzing and mining are going to be diverse, and it often depends on where you were able to get your data in the first place. Things like medical records, social network posts, call center logs, comments on surveys, emails from the customer, and even corporate documents can all be mined to figure out what important information is there.

Basically, anything that is full of text-based data that could also help the business to learn more about themselves, their customers, and their competition can be used in data mining.

There are a few different technologies that are going to come into play to help us sort through this information and make sure that it all fits together.

For example, in addition to working with the process of text mining, we can also work with artificial intelligence and natural language processing technologies to make sure that we are able to transform some of the key content that is found in various text documents into insights that are quantitative and actionable.

How Can Text Mining Help?

We have already spent a bit of time talking about the importance of text mining and what it is able to do for our business and all of the data that we are holding onto. Text mining is going to work in the same manner as we see with the process of data mining, but the focus is going to be more of the text rather than on the structured data. This makes it easier for us to handle and process a lot of the more complex and unstructured forms of data that most businesses are collecting in data science.

The first step that we need to do in the text mining process is to make sure that we can organize the data. We have to do this with regards to both quantitative and qualitative analysis. This is why we are going to bring out the technology for natural language processing to make this all work.

Text mining is going to include a few different parts that have to all come together to make sure that this process does what we are expecting. Some of the tasks that text mining are able to handle for us include:

1. Information identification and retrieval. This means that it is able to collect the data from all of the sources that you want to use and they will analyze it.

2. Apply the text analytics: This means that we are going to use different methods, including statistical methods or natural language processing to help with things like speed tagging.

3. Named entity recognition. This means that the program will be able to identify some of the

named text features the process name as categorizations.

4. Disambiguation. This means that we will focus on clustering.

5. Document clustering. This is used to help us identify sets of similar text documents.

6. Identify nouns and other terms that are going to end up referring to the same object, and then find out the relationship and the fact among the entities and some of the other information that is in the text.

7. Then we can perform a sentiment analysis as well as quantitative text analysis.

8. Finally, we can work to create an analytic model that is able to help us to generate the right business strategies and figure out the actions that we are able to take in here.

What Can Text Mining Do?

The best example that we are able to see with text mining is the sentimental analysis. This is an analysis that is able to track the review or the sentiment of a customer about a company and a product in a process that is known as opinion mining. In this kind of analysis, we are able to collect text from social networks, online reviews, and other sources of data and then perform our own NLP in order to identify the positive or the negative feedbacks that we see with the customers.

Another common use of all of this is going to be things like marketing to figure out how the customer will respond to things, biomedical applications to help with clinical studies, security applications, and even with things like fraud management in a bank or another financial institution.

We can even see this happen with scientific literature mining for a publisher to search through the data on an index retrieval system, how to classify a website, blocking out emails that are spam, figuring out when an insurance claim is going to be fraudulent, and examining some of the corporate documents that need to be looked over as part of the electronic discovery process.

The Advantages of Text Mining

The next thing that we need to take a look at is the advantages of text mining. There are a lot of benefits that come with using this kind of technique in your business and understanding how this works is going to make a big difference in your business and how you will work with text mining.

The first benefit is fraud detection. Insurance companies and banks will find that it can help with detecting fraud before this issue happens. It is a good way to figure out the behavior of your customers to determine which way to move your business. It can help with things like risk management so that the business is able to make some smart decisions that will actually benefit them rather than cause harm. And it can work with finishing up a scientific analysis as well.

This is just the beginning of what we are able to see when it comes to working with text mining though. In addition, text mining, when it is used with the right processes, can help a company to detect issues and then resolve these issues before they have the potential to become a big problem, which could negatively affect your company.

Text mining can help you to take a look at some of the communication and reviews from your customers in order to learn what the customer is telling us. Companies are then able to use this information to learn the best ways to improve the customer experience by identifying the features that are required for the customer.

It can also come in and help with other factors that are going to help to increase the sales and then the revenues and the profits of the company so that they can continue growing over time.

We can even take the idea of text mining a step further and see how we are able to use this in the healthcare industry. For example, this type of process is able to come into play to help us identify the diseases that a patient may have, and it could be a great way to diagnose a lot of the diseases, often before a doctor is able to do it.

More about Text Mining

To help us perform the process of text mining, it is important to have people on your team with skills for data analysis and have a good understanding of statistics. Other skills that the data scientist should have in order to complete this process including natural language processing, machine learning algorithms, deep learning algorithms, knowledge about how to work with databases, and information about frameworks of big data processing. It is also a good option to know how to program in a coding language as well to get some of the work done.

The scope of text mining is going to be interesting as well. Text mining is really a field that is growing like crazy, so the scope is promising in the future. The amount of text data is growing all of the time, and social media platforms are going to generate a lot of text data. We have to be able to mine all of this text data in order to get some real insights into the different domains that are present.

The target audience for working with and learning more about this technology is going to be professionals who would like to identify the valuable insights that the huge amount of unstructured data for companies for purposes that are varied. For example, it is possible for a company to use this to increase their sales and see more profits, to help with detecting fraud, to learn more about their customers, and to even perform scientific analysis that can put them in the lead of others.

In conclusion, there are a lot of different parts that we need to consider when it comes to text mining. Some of the things that we need to remember when it comes to this part of data science include:

1. Text mining is often going to be known as text data mining. This is the process of extracting and then analyzing data from a large amount of text data that is not structured.

2. Text mining work is going to include things like information retrieval or the identification of information, text analytics, named entity recognition, document clustering, identifying nouns or other keywords, and more among the information that we have in our text. We are then able to perform a sentiment analysis and a quantitative text analysis before creating an analytic model that will help to generate good business strategies that we can follow.

3. Text mining is going to help with things like healthcare, customer behavior, scientific analysis, risk management, and fraud detection to name a few

4. To help us perform this process of text mining, people need to have a variety of skill to get it done. This can include knowledge of deep learning and machine learning algorithms, natural language processing, database knowledge, big data processing frameworks, statistics, and data analysis.

5. It is a field is going to grow fast and will continue to do this as the field of big data continues to grow as well. This means that the scope that comes with text mining is promising in the future, and it is likely to continue growing more and more.

Working with text mining is going to be very important when we work with some of the unstructured data that comes up in our analysis. This process is going to help us to mine through the large amounts of text that we are working with, ensuring that we are able to see some results out of this data and that we are actually able to use it for our needs as well.

10. Variable Scope And Lifetime In Python Functions

Variables and parameters defined within a Python function have local scope implying they are not visible from outside. In Python, the variable lifetime is valid as long the function executes and is the period throughout that a variable exists in memory. Returning the function destroys the function variables.

Example

Start IDLE.

Navigate to the File menu and click New Window.

Type the following:

```
def function_my()

    marks=15

print("The value inside the function is:", marks)

marks=37

function_my()

Print"The value outside the function is:",marks)
```

Function Types

They are broadly grouped into user-defined and built-in functions. The built-in functions are part of the Python interpreter while the user-defined functions are specified by the user.

Exercise

Give three examples of built-in functions in Pythons

Function Argument

Calling a function requires passing the correct number of parameters otherwise the interpreter will generate an error.

Illustration

Start IDLE.

Navigate to the File menu and click New Window.

Type the following:

```
def salute(name,message):
    """This function welcomes to
    the student with the provided message"""
    print("Welcome",salute + ', ' + message)
```

welcome("Brenda","Lovely Day!")

Note: The function welcome() has two parameters. We will not get any error as has been fed with two arguments. Let us try calling the function with one argument and see what happens:

welcome("Brenda")   #only one argument passed

Running this program will generate an error saying "TypeError: welcome() missing 1 required positional argument. The same will happen when we pass no arguments to the function.

Example 2

Start IDLE.

Navigate to the File menu and click New Window.

Type the following:

welcome()

The interpreter will generate an error "typeerror: welcome() missing 2 required positional arguments".

Keywords Arguments in Python

Python provides a way of calling functions using keyword arguments. When calling functions using keyword arguments, the order of arguments can be changed. The values of a function are matched to the argument position-wise.

Note:

In the previous example function welcome when invoked as welcome("Brenda", "Lovely Day!"). The value "Brenda" is assigned to the argument name and "Lovely Day!" to msg.

Calling the function using keywords

Start IDLE.

Navigate to the File menu and click New Window.

Type the following:

welcome(name="Brenda", msg="Lovely Day!")

Keywords not following the order

Welcome(msg="Lovely Day!", name="Brenda")

Arbitrary Arguments

It may happen that we do not have knowledge of all arguments needed to be passed into a function. Analogy: Assume that you are writing a program to welcome all new students this semester. In this case, you do not how many will report.

Example

Start IDLE.

Navigate to the File menu and click New Window.

Type the following:

```
def welcome(*names):
    """This welcome function salutes all students in the names tuple."""
    for name in names:
        print("Welcome".name)
welcome("Lucy","Richard","Fridah","James")
```

The output of the program will be:

Welcome Lucy

Welcome Richard

Welcome Fridah

Welcome james

Recursion in Python

The definition of something in terms of itself is called recursion. A recursive function calls other functions.

Example

Python program to compute integer factorials

Start IDLE.

Navigate to the File menu and click New Window.

Type the following:

Exercise

Write a Python program to find the factorial of 7.

Python Anonymous Function

Some functions may be specified devoid of a name and these are called anonymous functions. The lambda keyword is used to denote an anonymous function. Anonymous functions are also referred to as lambda functions in Python.

Syntax

lambda arguments: expression.

Lambda functions must always have one expression but can have several arguments.

Example

Start IDLE.

Navigate to the File menu and click New Window.

Type the following:

```
double = lambda y: y * 2

# Output: 10

print(double(5))
```

Example 2

We can use inbuilt functions such as filter () and lambda to show only even numbers in a list/tuple.

Start IDLE.

Navigate to the File menu and click New Window.

Type the following:

```
first_marks = [3, 7, 14, 16, 18, 21, 13, 32]

fresh_marks = list(filter(lambda n: (n%2 == 0) ,
first_marks))

# Output: [14, 16, 18, 32]
```

print(fresh_marks)

Lambda function and map() can be used to double individual list items.

Example 3

Start IDLE.

Navigate to the File menu and click New Window.

Type the following:

first_score = [3, 7, 14, 16, 18, 21, 13, 32]

fresh_score = list(map(lambda m: m * 2 , first_score))

Output: [6, 14, 28, 32, 36, 42, 26, 64]

Print(fresh_score)

Python's Global, Local and Nonlocal

Python's Global Variables

Variables declared outside of a function in Python are known as global variables. They are declared in global scope. A global variable can be accessed outside or inside of the function.

Example

Start IDLE.

Navigate to the File menu and click New Window.

Type the following:

```
y= "global"
def foo():
    print("y inside the function :", y)
foo()
print("y outside the function:", y)
```

Explanation

In the illustration above, y is a global variable and is defined as a foo() to print the global variable y. When we call the foo() it will print the value of y.

Local Variables

 A local variable is declared within the body of the function or in the local scope.

Example

Start IDLE.

Navigate to the File menu and click New Window.

Type the following:

```
def foo():

    x = "local"

foo()

print(x)
```

Explanation

Running this program will generate an error indicating 'x' is undefined. The error is occurring because we are trying to access local variable x in a global scope whereas foo() functions only in the local scope.

Creating a Local Variable in Python

Example

A local variable is created by declaring a variable within the function.

```
def foo():
```

Start IDLE.

Navigate to the File menu and click New Window.

Type the following:

```
    x = "local"
```

```
    print(x)

foo()
```

Explanation

When we execute the code, the output will be:

Local

Python's Global and Local Variable

Using both local and global variables in the same code.

Example

Start IDLE.

Navigate to the File menu and click New Window.

Type the following:

```
y = "global"

def foo():

    global y

    x = "local"

    y = y * 2

    print(y)
```

```
    print(x)
```

```
foo()
```

Explanation

The output of the program will be:

global global

local

Explanation

We declared y as a global variable and x as a local variable in the foo(). The * operator issued to modify the global variable y and finally, we printed both y and x.

Local and Global Variables with the same name

Start IDLE.

Navigate to the File menu and click New Window.

Type the following:

```
y=6
```

```
def foo():
```

```
y=11
```

```
    print("Local variable y-", y)
```

foo()

Print("Global variable y-", y)

Python's Nonlocal Variables

 A Python's nonlocal variable is used in a nested function whose local scope is unspecified. It is neither global nor local scope.

Example

Creating a nonlocal variable.

Start IDLE.

Navigate to the File menu and click New Window.

Type the following:

```
def outer():

    y = "local variable"

    def inner():

        nonlocal y

        y = "nonlocal variable"

        print("inner:", y)
```

    inner()

    print("outer scope:", y)

Outer()

Global Keyword in Python

There are rules when creating a global keyword:

A global keyword is local by default when we create a variable within a function.

It is global by default when we define a variable outside of a function and you do not need to use the global keyword.

The global keyword is used to read and write a global variable within a function.

The use of global keyword outside a function will have no effect.

Example.

Start IDLE.

Navigate to the File menu and click New Window.

Type the following:

```python
number = 3        #A global variable

def add():

    print(number)

add()
```

The output of this program will be 3.

Modifying global variable from inside the function.

```python
number=3                    #a global variable

def add():

    number= number + 4    # add 4 to 3

    print(number)

add()
```

Explanation

When the program is executed it will generate an error indicating that the local variable number is referenced before assignment. The reason for encountering the error is because we can only access the global variable but are unable to modify it from inside the function. Using a global keyword would solve this.

Example.

Start IDLE.

Navigate to the File menu and click New Window.

Type the following:

Modifying global variable within a function using the global keyword.

```
number = 3          # a global variable
def add():
    global number
    number= number + 1 # increment by 1
    print("Inside the function add():", number)
add()
print("In main area:", number)
```

Explanation

When the program is run, the output will be:

 Inside the function add(): 4

In the main area: 4

We defined a number as a global keyword within the function add(). The variable was then incremented by 1, variable number. Then we called the add () function to print global variable c.

Creating Global Variables across Python Modules

We can create a single module config.py that will contain all global variables and share the information across several modules within the same program.

Example.

Start IDLE.

Navigate to the File menu and click New Window.

Type the following:

Create config.py

x=0

y="empty"

Then create an update.py file to modify global variables

Import config

config.x=11

config.y="Today"

Then create a main.py file to evaluate the changes in value

import config

import update

print(config.x)

print(config.y)

Explanation

Running the main.py file will generate:

11

Today

Python Modules

Modules consist of definitions as well as program statements.

An illustration is a file name config.py which is considered as a module. The module name would be config. Modules are sued to help break large programs into smaller manageable and organized files as well as promoting reusability of code.

Example: Creating the First module

Start IDLE.

Navigate to the File menu and click New Window.

Type the following:

Def add(x, y):

"""This is a program to add two

   numbers and return the outcome"""

outcome=x+y

return outcome

Module Import

The keyword import is used to import.

Example

Import first

The dot operator can help us access a function as long as we know the name of the module.

Example

Start IDLE.

Navigate to the File menu and click New Window.

Type the following:

first.add(6,8)

Explanation

import statement in Python

The import statement can be used to access the definitions within a module via the dot operator.

Start IDLE.

Navigate to the File menu and click New Window.

Type the following:

import math

print("The PI value is", math.pi)

Import with renaming

Example

Start IDLE.

Navigate to the File menu and click New Window.

Type the following:

import math as h

```
print("The PI value is-",h.pi)
```

Explanation

In this case, h is our renamed math module with a view helping save typing time in some instances. When we rename the new name becomes valid and recognized one and not the original one.

From...import statement Python.

It is possible to import particular names from a module rather than importing the entire module.

Example

Start IDLE.

Navigate to the File menu and click New Window.

Type the following:

from math import pi

Print("The PI value is-", pi)

Importing all names

Example

Start IDLE.

Navigate to the File menu and click New Window.

Type the following:

```
from math import*
print("The PI value is-", pi)
```

Explanation

In this context, we are importing all definitions from a particular module but it is encouraged norm as it can lead to unseen duplicates.

Module Search Path in Python

Example

Start IDLE.

Navigate to the File menu and click New Window.

Type the following:

```
import sys
sys.path
```

Python searches everywhere including the sys file.

Reloading a Module

Python will only import a module once increasing efficiency in execution.

print("This program was executed")

import mine

Reloading Code

Example

Start IDLE.

Navigate to the File menu and click New Window.

Type the following:

import mine

import mine

import mine

Mine.reload(mine)

Dir() built-in Python function

For discovering names contained in a module, we use the dir() inbuilt function.

Syntax

Dir(module_name)

Python Package

Files in python hold modules and directories are stored in packages. A single package in Python holds similar modules. Therefore, different modules should be placed in different Python packages.

Data types in Python

☐   Numbers

The presence or absence of a decimal point separates integers and floating points. For instance, 4 is integer while 4.0 is a floating point number.

On the other hand, complex numbers in Python are denoted as r+tj where j represents the real part and t is the virtual part. In this context, the function type() is used to determine the variable class. The Python function instance() is invoked to make a determination of which specific class function originates from.

Example

Start IDLE.

Navigate to the File menu and click New Window.

Type the following:

number=6

```
  print(type(number))#should output class int
```

print(type(6.0))#should output class float

complex_num=7+5j

print(complex_num+5)

print(isinstance(complex_num, complex))#should output True

Important: Integers in Python can be of infinite length. Floating numbers in Python are assumed precise up to fifteen decimal places.

Number Conversion

This segment assumes you have prior basic knowledge of how to manually or using a calculator to convert decimal into binary, octal and hexadecimal. Check out the Windows Calculator in Windows 10, Calculator version Version 10.1804.911.1000 and choose programmer mode to automatically convert.

Programmers often need to convert decimal numbers into octal, hexadecimal and binary forms. A prefix in Python allows denotation of these numbers to their corresponding type.

Number SystemPrefix

Octal`0O' or '0o'

Binary`0B' or '0b'

Hexadecimal'0X or '0x'

Example

print(0b1010101)#Output:85

print(0x7B+0b0101)#Output: 128 (123+5)

print(0o710)#Output:710

Exercise

Write a Python program to display the following:

a.0011 11112

b.7478

C.9316

Type Conversion

Sometimes referred to as coercion, type conversion allows us to change one type of number into another. The preloaded functions such as float(), int() and complex() enable implicit and explicit type conversions. The same functions can be used to change from strings.

Example

Start IDLE.

Navigate to the File menu and click New Window.

Type the following:

int(5.3)#Gives 5

int(5.9)#Gives 5

The int() will produce a truncation effect when applied to floating numbers. It will simply drop the decimal point part without rounding off. For the float() let us take a look:

Start IDLE.

Navigate to the File menu and click New Window.

Type the following:

float(6)#Gives 6.0

ccomplex('4+2j')#Gives (4+2j)

Exercise

Apply the int() conversion to the following:

a.4.1

b.4.7

c.13.3

d.13.9

Apply the float() conversion to the following:

e.7

f.16

G.19

□   *Decimal in Python*

Example

Start IDLE.

Navigate to the File menu and click New Window.

Type the following:

(1.2+2.1)==3.3 #Will return False, why?

Explanation

The computer works with finite numbers and fractions cannot be stored in their raw form as they will create an infinite long binary sequence.

□   *Fractions in Python*

The fractions module in Python allows operations on fractional numbers.

Example

Start IDLE.

Navigate to the File menu and click New Window.

Type the following:

import fractions

print(fractions.my_fraction(2.5))#Output 5/2

print(fractions.my_fraction(4))#Output 5

print(fractions.my_fraction(2,5))#output 2/5

Important

Creating my_fraction from float can lead to unusual results due to the misleading representation of binary floating point.

Mathematics in Python

To carry out mathematical functions, Python offers modules like random and math.

Start IDLE.

Navigate to the File menu and click New Window.

Type the following:

import math

print(math.pi)#output:3.14159....

print(math.cos(math.pi))#the output will be -1.0

print(math.exp(10))#the output will be 22026.4....

print(math.log10(100))#the output will be 2

print(math.factorial(5))#the output will be 120

Exercise

Write a python program that uses math functions from the math module to perform the following:

a.Square of 34

b.Log1010000

c.Cos 45 x sin 90

D.Exponent of 20

Random function in Python

Start IDLE.

Navigate to the File menu and click New Window.

Type the following:

import math

print(random.shuffle_num(11, 21))

y=['f','g','h','m']

print(random.pick(y))

random.anypic(y)

print(y)

Print(your_pick.random())

Lists in Python

We create a list in Python by placing items called elements inside square brackets separated by commas. The items in a list can be of mixed data types.

Start IDLE.

Navigate to the File menu and click New Window.

Type the following:

list_mine=[]#empty list

list_mine=[2,5,8]#list of integers

list_mine=[5,"Happy", 5.2]#list having mixed data types

Exercise

Write a program that captures the following in a list: "Best", 26,89,3.9

Nested Lists

A nested list is a list as an item in another list.

Example

Start IDLE.

Navigate to the File menu and click New Window.

Type the following:

list_mine=["carrot", [9, 3, 6], ['g']]

Exercise

Write a nested for the following elements:
[36,2,1],"Writer",'t',[3.0, 2.5]

Accessing Elements from a List

In programming and in Python specifically, the first time is always indexed zero. For a list of five items, we will access them from index0 to index4. Failure to access the items in a list in this manner will create index error. The index is always an integer as using other number types will create a type error. For nested lists, they are accessed via nested indexing.

Example

Start IDLE.

Navigate to the File menu and click New Window.

Type the following:

list_mine=['b','e','s','t']

print(list_mine[0])#the output will be b

print(list_mine[2])#the output will be s

print(list_mine[3])#the output will be t

Exercise

Given the following list:

your_collection=['t','k','v','w','z','n','f']

a.Write a Python program to display the second item in the list

b.Write a Python program to display the sixth item in the last

C.Write a Python program to display the last item in the list.

11. Future Of Python

Increasing Popularity of Python

Python is ruling the world of modern technology and due to its uniqueness it has left other languages like C++, Java, etc. far behind. Python, with its great utility, has a promising and bright future. Python has gone though 25 years of continuous amendments with improved and better-updated versions so that it can serve as the fastest and most reliable programming language. Python provides the best quality, which is why it catches the eye of every developer. Over 126,000 websites have utilized Python. A plethora of decision-making systems for predictive analysis have developed applications using Python. It is the language of today and the future, as well.

Profiles of Python developers

Python developers are as assorted as the language and its applications. Python clients vary broadly in age, yet most of its users are in their 20s, and a quarter are in their 30s. Strikingly, nearly one-fifth of Python clients are under the age of 20. It can be clarified, by the way, that numerous under-studies use Python in schools and colleges, and it's a common first language for many computer programmers.

According to the recent survey, almost 65% of software engineers are moving towards Python language as a career. As Python is a simple and easy to learn language, many newcomers are adopting this high-level language to make their fortune from this new field of Data Science. It is a widespread practice nowadays and every software engineer is looking to learn the libraries, methods, and use of Python to become a data scientist. 30% of engineers that have under two years of expert experience have started using Python as their primary programming language.

General Python utilization

Right around four out of five Python designers state it's their primary language. Different research demonstrates the quantity of Python engineers, which are using it as primary language. In Stack Overflow's review, Python fame has expanded from 32% in mid-2017 to 38.8% by the end of that year.

Python utility with Other Languages:

Python is being used by all developers now who were only focusing on other high-level languages just a year ago. This trend is changing because of the evolution of Data Science.

According to a survey, JavaScript is utilized by 79% of web engineers, yet just 39% of those are engaged with Data investigation or Artificial Intelligence.

Some important companies that use Python as Data Science:

Google

Google is considered the biggest IT giant and has supported Python from its start. Google utilizes Python in their web crawler.

Facebook

Facebook is keen in utilizing Python in their Production Engineering Department.

Instagram

Instagram's engineering team revealed in 2016 that the world's most massive deployment of the Django web framework driven by them is completely written in Python.

Netflix

Netflix utilizes Python in a very similar manner to Spotify, depending on the language to power its data analysis on the server-side.

Dropbox

This cloud-based storage system employs Python in its desktop client.

10.2 Factors behind the Python growth in Modern World

Growth of Python is becoming prominent and is improving day by day. Software engineers and developers prefer this language due to its versatility and ease of use. Various other factors that are behind its growth are as follows:

1. Good support and community

Programming languages often face support issues. They lack complete documentation to help programmers when problems arise. Python has no such issues and is well supported. A plethora of tutorials and documentation is available to assist the programmers in the best possible ways. It has a good and active community whose function is to support developers. Experienced programmers help the beginners and a supportive atmosphere has been created.

2. Easy to Code and Write

If we compare Python to other programming languages like Java, C or C++, Python possesses a readable and straightforward code. Coding is expressed in a relatively easy manner to allow beginners to understand it quickly.

To learn the advanced level of python programming, a lot of time and effort is required, but for beginners, it is an easy task. Users can quickly identify the purpose of code, even after a quick glance.

3. Python is the Language of Education

Python is an easy language to use. It possesses functions, expressions, variables, and all other elements that students can easily understand and practice. It is the standard programming language for the Raspberry Pi, a PC structured training. Colleges teach Python in PC sciences, as well as to arithmetic understudies. Also,

Matplotlib (a prominent Python library) is utilized in subjects at all levels to express complex data. Python is one of the quickest developing languages on Codecademy, as well, and thus is anything but difficult to learn remotely.

4. Simple to Code and Write

Python has an elementary coding and syntax structure. In comparison to other high-level programming languages like Java, C, or C++, Python has a straightforward and discernible code. The code is communicated in a simple way, which can be mostly deciphered even by a novice software engineer.

5. Python Is Perfect For Building Prototypes.

Python not only allows the users to write less code, it also provides the utility to build prototypes and ideas very quickly. Brainstorming or ideation is an essential aspect of web development, which is mostly overlooked. The capability to think about prototypes that can function faster becomes much more pivotal.

4. Integration and execution is quick

Python is considered as high-class language. It is the quickest language when it comes to execution and integration and saves quite a lot of time for programmers. With projects like PyPy and Numba, the speed is enhanced even more, making it the fastest language with each passing day.

5. Python has a Standard Library

Python contains libraries that eliminate the burden of composing a code by the programmer. These libraries possess a large quantity of built-in functions and already available codes. Therefore, code can easily be generated instead of having to be created.

6. Cross-Platform Language

One of the most prominent features of Python Programming Language is that it is accessible to cross-platforms. It supports highly efficient operating systems such as Linux, Windows, Ubuntu, and more.

Thus, one can undoubtedly keep running a product without agonizing over framework support. It very well may be translated in the language with the assistance of a convenient component that makes it easy to utilize. To sum things up - compose code on the Mac and run it smoothly on Windows.

7. Provides a plethora of tools

It contains a vast standard library collection, which reduce the effort for writing codes or functions. Libraries in Python always have pre-written codes in them.

Some of the tools are as follows: Tkinter (a GUI development), file format, built-in function, custom Python interpreter, internet protocols and support, module, etc. This extensive collection increases the usefulness of Python as a programming tool for data science.

8. Python is Free

Python is an open-source language and its free to use. Guido van Rossum has run Python since its creation. It is Open Source and GPL excellent. The creator of this language had a vision to keep it free for all the programmers of the world. However, open-source programming has officially changed the world. Python has no hidden cost or sale-able modules, and this makes it an ideal device for all to utilize.

9. Career Opportunities Associated With Python

In this powerful present-day world where everything changes at a quick rate, the prevalence of Python never seems to stop. Today, Python Certification is very popular. It has a lot of libraries that help data investigation, control, and representation. In this manner, it has advanced as the most favored language and viewed as the "Following Big Thing" and an "Absolute necessity" for Professionals.

With a wide range of programming languages, Python has outperformed different languages. Vocation openings related to Python have additionally developed fundamentally as its fame has expanded. Numerous IT organizations are searching for more applicants with experience and aptitudes in Python programming languages. Python has shown to be the best vocation for software engineers and now is the time - sooner rather than later.

Conclusion

We have covered the basics of Python programming language. The constructs we have learned so far, such as loops, expressions, and conditions, should be enough to help you further your career in Python development. What we have covered is enough to help you understand Python examples.

Although not everything has been covered, we have tried to provide you with a refresher in Python that you can build on it to become an excellent programmer. Python is one of the top four widely used programming language. As it has increased in popularity, its main focus on the quality of code and readability, plus the associated impact on developer productivity, appears to have been the driving force to Python success.

If you experience difficulties with some of the concepts discussed in this book, it is good if you can explore other introductory resources to help you understand. Or you can even consult with an experienced Python developer.

In general, you should master the basics of python discussed inside this book, master the language syntax, and then start to deepen your knowledge on specific features of python. Keep in mind that great programmers don't stop learning. So make a point always to learn something new in Python every day.

www.ingramcontent.com/pod-product-compliance
Lightning Source LLC
LaVergne TN
LVHW051226050326
832903LV00028B/2261